The Greatest MENTORS
IN · THE · BIBLE

32
RELATIONSHIPS
God Used to Change the World

By Tim Elmore

A DEVOTIONAL GUIDE

CONTENTS

Mentoring,
Then & Now

I don't think I'll ever forget watching the evening news during the summer of 1995. It was during those sticky, hellish months that America experienced an unbelievable heat wave. Chicago, in particular, was especially hard hit. Hundreds of people died from absolute heat exhaustion. The news footage was most depressing, one night in August. After reporting the number of lives that were lost due to the heat, the news commentator mentioned that forty one bodies were left, with no one to claim them. They were the corpses of people who died, but had no family or friends—*or anyone* to come and give them a decent burial. They couldn't find anyone who knew them enough to care. These people were among the rising number of Americans who've become completely detached from society. Anti-social behavior isn't limited to criminals. Some of these "friendless" people are not *bad* people; they have simply drifted from any accountable relationships in their life. Intimacy, commitment and accountability are too much work for them.

After writing my book, *Soul Provider*, I spoke to a woman on a radio talk show. She had called in to comment on my challenge (during the program) to spiritual leaders to "assume responsibility for the health of their relationships." I can still hear her voice. "I could never do what you've just instructed us to do," she said. "I've determined I am going to live the life of a hermit. It is so much easier to just care for myself, and not get involved in everyone else's dysfunction." She paused. "Don't you agree?"

I was stunned. Of course I agreed; it is easier not to get involved. But, the scripture doesn't leave that option open to us. *People* are what our faith is all about. According to a team of scholars, this is what separates Christianity from the religions of the world. This team of theologians met years ago in an attempt to summarize the Christian faith into one phrase. No doubt, this was to be quite a feat. They actually took it one step further. They distilled the faith into one, simple word. That word is: "relationships." Relationships with God (vertical) and with one another (horizontal). Jesus said, "Do this in remembrance of *me*" not "my teaching." He also said, "Who do you say that I am?" not "What do you think about my doctrine?" Interestingly, he also clarified: "By this will all men know that you are my disciples—if you love one another." He didn't say it was by memorizing creeds or scripture. Our faith is all about relationships. I believe God created us human beings with not only a "God shaped vacuum" inside of us, as Augustine has written, but also with a "people shaped vacuum" as well. We need God; and we need each other.

TRENDS TODAY...

Perhaps this is why we see what we are seeing in our society today. While some have determined it is easier to walk away from marriages and friendships, others have begun to cry out for these kinds of intimate relationships. "Partnership" is one of the big words of the '90s. Generation X would rather have quality relationships than high-tech productions in their churches. What's more, they are beginning to express their longing to be taught and guided in a mentoring relationship as well. As I have traveled over the last ten years, I have seen churches full of "Timothys" looking for "Pauls" to mentor them. People want a "coach" more than a "classroom;" they want a listening ear more than a lecture. In short, I believe people (however fearful and hesitant they may appear) long for intimate, steady, accountable, mentoring relationships today—and they don't quite know how to find them.

Fortunately for them, their cry has begun to be heard. Clearly, another buzzword of the '90s is the word: mentoring. The idea is no longer a secret.

The idea and the art of mentoring has really caught on in our generation. This has led to churches rediscovering the one to one discipleship model; it has led to Christian colleges creating mentor match ups between students and professors; it has led to relational structures being established in small group ministries; and, it has even led to junior executives seeking out mentors in the lunchrooms of corporate America. Because the culture of our time has recognized the vacuum of relationships that exists, people are crying out everywhere for mentors. The climate is right for learning through relationships.

MENTORING IN DAYS GONE BY...

Interestingly, this is not a new concept. While Americans have embraced the "greek" model for learning, the "hebrew" model has been employed by God's people for centuries, especially during the days of the Bible. The "greek" model I have referred to, is what I simply call the "classroom" model. This takes place when a teacher assumes his/her place up front, and the students sit passively to listen to a lecture. It is academic in nature; it is cerebral and cognitive. It is passive. And, while it is the fastest method to transfer information to another person or group—it is not the most effective method for the student to learn. Learning happens much more efficiently through the "hebrew" model, where the teacher or "mentor" invites the student(s) to travel with him/her. The hebrews learned through developmental relationships. No doubt, the mentor has much to say through verbal *instruction*, but this is not the only tool in their pocket. They *demonstrate* the principles or truths they want their mentorees to embrace. Then, they let those mentorees try their hand at it themselves. They understand that the best way to learn is to *experience* something firsthand. Finally, they give time for debriefing and feedback. They provide *accountability* and assessment. Notice the contrast below:

Two Learning Methods	
Greek	**Hebrew**
"Classroom Model"	*"Coach Model"*
• Academic	• Relational
• Passive	• Experiential
• Cerebral/Informational	• On-The-Job Training

These two learning methods received their titles from the culture in which they were popularized. Long before Jesus came along and chose twelve to mentor, the ancient Greek culture was making disciples. Socrates discipled Plato. Plato discipled Aristotle. Aristotle discipled Alexander the Great. But mentoring was much more philosophical in nature than the Hebrew model. It was more academic than relational. It was more passive than experiential. It was, in fact, much more like the classrooms of our schools and churches across the United States than what Jesus did with his disciples.

Jesus treated his disciples or mentorees more like *apprentices*, than academians. Theirs was "on-the-job training" and you can imagine how that must have accelerated their learning curve. Can you visualize how much more quickly Simon Peter must have grasped how Jesus cast out demons or how he spoke truth to a tax collector when he knew Jesus was going to ask him to do it the following week?

Down through the years, this kind of mentoring relationship has proven effective in both business and in faith. When I think of what mentoring looked like in England and Europe two or three hundred years ago, a certain image comes to mind. I can see cobblestone streets, lined with shops on both sides. Can you see it, too? I see shingles hanging from those shops, displaying where the blacksmith works, where the silversmith works, where the shoemaker works, and so on. Inside, there is purposeful activity. And if you look closely, you will see—not just the master blacksmith at work—but also an apprentice, as well. This apprentice is younger and less experienced. That's why he is there. He is observing and learning all he can. He is attempting to perfect what the "master" has shown him, because one day, if his plans and dreams come true, he will own a shop of his own. He will turn around and not only produce goods and services for the community, but he will have an apprentice on hand to mentor, himself!

What a beautiful and practical snapshot of the mentoring process. Throughout biblical history, we see this process as well, time and time again. Relationships formed. Eventually, they became *developmental relationships*. For many of the men and women of the Bible, these mentoring relationships were natural. It was a father mentoring his son. If you remember, Jesus worked as a carpenter under his stepfather Joseph until he was thirty years old, according to historians. Fathers would bless their sons with affirming words spoken at crucial times in their growth. Jacob, for instance, spoke specific words of blessing and future direction over all twelve of his sons. He even assigned the name of an *animal* (or object) to each, as a word of vision for their future success. Judah was a lion. Issachar was a donkey. Naphtali was a doe. Dan was a snake. This spoken word was all part of the "blessing" given to Jewish boys from their fathers, as a part of the tradition among Jews. As dads did this kind of mentoring, it obviously, reduced the need for outside mentoring in their son's adult lives. Tutors were also used in their children's earlier years. These were sort of "personal teachers," an early form of home schooling, you might say. Relationship structures were simple and precise within Hebrew families.

Clearly, the Jewish culture was an extremely relational culture. In our culture today, we commonly pose this question to college students: "What classes are you taking?" or "What subjects are you studying?" In the Hebrew culture, they would ask: "Who are you studying under?" The focus was on the mentor not the material. In the book of Hebrews we are exhorted to continue in this relational venue, as God's people. In Hebrews 10:24-25 we read that we are to "stimulate" each other; to "continue to meet together" and to "encourage" each other. It is interesting to note that the word "paraclete" is used here in this text. That is the same word Jesus used to describe the Holy Spirit who would come to help us in our walk with God! It literally means to "come alongside to help." What a picture of a mentor.

FINDING THE RIGHT MENTOR AND MENTOREE

I have recommended for years, as others have done, that each of us need a **Paul** and a **Barnabas**, and a **Timothy** in our lives. This means we will provide the best chance for spiritual health in our lives if we have a mentor who is ahead of us; a peer mentor or accountability partner who is beside us; and a mentoree who is following us. This three-fold relationship structure gives incentive to us, since we have someone who is overseeing our lives; as well as someone who is watching from behind, in order to imitate us. If you cannot think of a person who fills those roles for you, why not stop right now and ask God to provide them for you. Jot their names down, as He brings them to your mind.

In their insightful book, *Connecting*, Robert Clinton and Paul Stanley outline the seven different kinds of mentors that most often exist in our lives. It is important for us to examine these seven roles to determine which we most *need,* as well as to discern which we are most suited to *become* for someone else. Knowing your personal style and your gifts will enable you to better decide what kind of mentor you need for yourself, and can become for someone else. Note these seven kinds of mentors below:

1. DISCIPLER...............Helping with the basics of following Christ
2. SPIRITUAL GUIDE.....Accountability; direction/insight for maturation
3. COACH.............Motivation; skills needed to meet a task/challenge
4. COUNSELOR....Timely advice; perspective on self, others, ministry
5. TEACHER...............Knowledge/understanding of a specific subject
6. SPONSOR........Career guidance; protection; relational networking
7. MODEL...........A living, personal example for life, ministry, career

You will observe that each of these different roles provides a different kind of service to someone. Some are best suited for close, regular inspections of the spiritual life of a mentoree. Others serve more as a "consultant" where the meetings between the mentoree and mentor are less frequent. This table of various mentor roles is helpful and liberating. First, because it prevents us from some unrealistic pursuit of one, ideal mentor, or a pursuit to become one, ideal, perfect mentor. Second, it can help all of us see which role we are best suited for. Third, it serves as a guide for us in the different stages of our lives. We will need different kinds of mentors in different places in our ministry or career. All of us need a "brain to pick, a shoulder to cry on, and a kick in the seat of the pants."

In his excellent motion picture, *Mr. Holland's Opus*, Richard Dryfuss plays the role of a musician who desperately wants to compose music and become famous. He is very honest about this yearning, early in the story. He winds up becoming a high school teacher to save some money until he and his wife can move away and fulfill his dreams. Somewhere in route, his values change. Almost against his will, he becomes a *mentor* for many of these students, not just their classroom teacher. He invests extra time, after class, with them. He gives them personal time and direction. He persists in his belief in them, until many of them become "somebody" following their graduation.

Toward the end of the film, Mr. Holland is forced to resign due to cutbacks in the school budget. He moans to a colleague that "just the time you think you've really made a difference to people"— you get hit with a reality check. He is depressed and frightened, not knowing what to do next and not knowing if he has made a poor decision by staying a teacher, instead of pursuing fame and fortune. It is at that moment that the story climaxes. He is walking out of the school building for the last time, when he hears students singing in the auditorium. He opens the door, and finds hundreds and hundreds of his former students who have returned to say "thanks" for his investment in them. A group of graduates play the one concerto he has found time to write, as a teacher. He cannot fight back the tears as he is smitten with the overwhelming results of his investment in the lives of his "mentorees" and to see the adults they have become. The deposits he had made over time had now paid great dividends.

This is a picture of mentoring. Many of his students were, in their own way, crying out for a mentor. He resisted at first, as many of us do. The relationships that emerged, however, demonstrate what a valuable investment he had made—pouring into people, not just his own career. Instead of gaining a few years of fame at a nightclub or even on Broadway—he left a legacy behind him, of people who are changing their world.

Do You Need A Mentor?

Obviously, I don't know the stage of life you are experiencing now. However, I am certain that all of us, whatever stage we are facing—benefit from someone who is further along than we are, to walk us through our own journey. Let me pose a question to you:

Would You Like To Be Mentored By One Or More Of The Greatest Leaders In The Bible?

This devotional guide will give you that opportunity! You will get to meet these individuals and watch them operate in a mentoring context. You will see snapshots of these leaders speaking into the lives of people who struggle with the same things you do; people who share the same needs, who are tempted with the same sins, and are faced with the same kinds of challenges we face today.

Whether you need a model to follow as a mentoree, or you need a model to follow as you mentor someone yourself—these profiles of men and women will give you a headstart in the process. They will provide both principles and pictures of what makes mentoring work, and how you can do it with excellence today. You will see both successes and failures as you read these pages. You will see long term mentoring relationships and short term relationships. You will see both old and young; male and female; single and married; rich and poor; famous and faceless hebrews—who simply knew that they needed *others* in their life if they were going to reach their potential.

In the next chapter we will examine one more important part of the process, before I turn you loose to study these great mentors. We will observe just how a mentor or mentoree is selected, and what is supposed to happen (ideally) in this journey we call: **mentoring.**

THE
MENTORING
JOURNEY

At this point in my life, I have intentionally mentored almost two hundred people, either one to one, or in a small group. I have failed as often as I have succeeded, in being and doing what my mentoree really needed at the moment. I have cringed and cried when I've thought about some of my earlier days in ministry—attempting to "pour my life" into someone, but not knowing just how to do it. Thank God for merciful mentorees, who were just happy to gain whatever they could from someone like me. In most cases, my mentorees did proceed to turn around and mentor someone else, just as I had done with them. It has been most fulfilling to watch this take place.

As I have reflected on my past mentoring experience, I have noticed that two questions consistently emerge from those I have worked with. Usually at the beginning of the journey, these two questions are on the minds of both the mentor and the mentoree. The two questions are:

1. How do I go about selecting a mentor or mentoree?

2. What exactly is supposed to happen in a mentoring relationship?

In this preliminary chapter, let's attempt to answer these two questions in a succinct yet helpful fashion. I trust that after addressing these issues, we will have laid a foundation for *you* to enter the mentoring journey...for the rest of your life. Remember—your own *application* of these truths is the paramount issue on God's heart. I trust it is with you as well. Let's begin with a look at the selection process.

THE PROCESS OF SELECTING A MENTOR OR MENTOREE

I am frequently struck by the simplicity of how Jesus selected his twelve disciples or "mentorees" in the Gospels. It appears that He simply prayed all night, then chose a handful of men—from scratch! What's more, it seems as though they just up and left their work and followed Him, without any prior knowledge of what they were in for. Oh, if it were only that easy today, we sigh. If only we could find a mentor with that much authority and credibility; or— if only we could get people to follow our mentoring that quickly and simply.

Upon closer study, we discover that it really *wasn't* that easy, even for Jesus. No doubt, there was a time when He did issue a challenge to Peter, James and John to follow Him, and they did, indeed, leave their nets to follow. I do not believe, however, that this was their first exposure to Jesus, or His call on their life. I believe there was a PROCESS involved, that required several *stages* of relationship. My good friend Steve Moore and I have attempted to assign titles to these stages of mentoring relationships to help you see the process necessary for people to enter, in order to make the kind of commitment that mentoring requires. I share this with you to liberate you from unrealistic expectations, and to give you a path to take, as you enter the process yourself. Let me outline this process for you.

COME AND SEE...

This is stage one. In the Gospel of John, we see Jesus' first encounter with his potential disciples or "mentorees." In John 1:35-51 a conversation begins when Jesus discovers that two of John the Baptizer's disciples are following Him. He asks them what they are seeking. They inquire where He is staying. They are obviously at a **curiosity level.** They just want to know a little bit more about Him, and what it means to be associated with Him. After all, this is a new experience. All He says in response is: "Come and see." For us, this may mean offering an opportunity to a potential mentoree to observe some ministry in action; or to spend some time with us, personally—just to get acquainted. If you are going to win their trust, you need to give them time. By offering these opportunities, you are demonstrating *first* your commitment and intentions to them. The commitment level is low, and the challenge is simple and easy. Your relationship may even be in its early stages. Your appropriate call on their life is simply: come and see.

COME AND FOLLOW...

This is stage two. At this stage, Jesus believes His disciples are ready to actually make a commitment, and follow after Him, as a mentor. This is precisely what many of the twelve were after. Some of them, at this point, are not ready to call Him "Lord." He is "teacher" to them. In Luke 5:1-11, Simon Peter doesn't even feel comfortable being *close* to Jesus, and tells Him to depart from the area. Peter realized what an unworthy man he was, and that the Lord Himself was standing in front of him. Jesus knew he was ready for stage two, however, and simply said, "Do not fear, from now on you will be catching men." In Matthew 4:19, His words are put this way: "Come, follow me, and I will make you fishers of men." These kinds of words are to be spoken to those ready for the **commitment level** who are ready to sacrifice in order to go forward and grow further. The word "follow" means "repeated, deliberate steps." Everyone is not ready for this level of commitment to a mentoring process. At this stage, mentorees prove themselves to be faithful to the little tasks and assignments given by the mentor. They are willing to "follow the ruts of routine until they have become grooves of grace," as Dr. Vernon Grounds has put it. For us, these routines might be faithfulness to meeting together; or reading books that you will later discuss together; or performing a ministry task; or keeping a journal; or fasting; etc., etc.

At this stage, the mentoree is clearly prepared to follow the mentor, deliberately.

COME AND SURRENDER...

This is stage three. Somewhere in the midst of Jesus' three

and a half year ministry to the twelve, He issued a deeper challenge
to them as mentorees. In a word, you might say He asked them to
"die;" to make the ultimate commitment. In Mark 8:34-35 He
said: "If anyone wishes to come after Me, let him deny himself,
take up his cross, and follow Me. For whoever wishes to save his
life shall lose it; but whoever loses his life for My sake and the
gospel's shall save it." This kind of call is appropriate for those at
the **conviction level.** If a person is not ready to take this deep and
heavy step—it will become clear by their reaction. Do you remember the rich, young ruler? Jesus asked him to sell everything he had
(something He did not ask everyone He met to do!) and to come
follow Him. The young man, who thought he was further along in
his spiritual journey than he was, just dropped his head and walked
away. The step was too big for him to take. For us, at this stage,
the mentoree has so bought into the mentor that they not only love
him/her, but *the cause* as well. They are prepared to give their life
to the mission. Profound steps of action can be expected from the
mentoree because the maturity level is deep. It is very appropriate,
then, to issue a challenge: come and surrender.

COME AND MULTIPLY...

This is the fourth stage. During the latter part of Jesus'
mentoring relationship with the twelve, He began to send them out
to do it themselves. In fact, the final words He spoke to them are
called "the Great Commission." In Matthew 28:19-20 we read:
"Go and make disciples of all nations, baptizing them...and teaching them to obey all that I've commanded you..." In Mark 16 His
words are: "Go into all the world and preach the Gospel to every
creature..." In John 20:21 He said, "As the Father has sent Me, so
I send you." They were to duplicate what He had just done with
them as mentorees. This is the **commissioned level.** We're to go
full circle. At this point, the mentoree is ready to become a mentor.
If they are to continue stretching and growing, they must be "pushed
out of the nest" and made to fly. They must pass on what they've
received; they must imitate the process and duplicate the lifestyle.
They must reproduce themselves. Unfortunately, very few ever

reach this level. Many stop and are satisfied merely being mentored. But Jesus said, "Freely you have received, freely give." He also issued this final call to us: come and multiply.

FINDING THE RIGHT PERSON

In my book, *Mentoring: How To Invest Your Life in Others*, I spent a couple of chapters on how to find a "mentor" and how to find a "mentoree." Let me give you a summary of those chapters. These are the qualities I look for, in both mentors and mentorees: If you are a mentor—you need to develop G.O.A.L.S. If you are a mentoree—you need to have F.A.I.T.H. Note the following qualities...

Mentors Must Have...	Mentorees Must Have...
G-Godliness	**F**-Faithfulness
O-Objectivity	**A**-Availability
A-Authenticity	**I**-Initiative
L-Loyalty	**T**-Teachability
S-Servanthood	**H**-Hunger

I trust that these lists will help you locate the right person for you. In the pages that follow you will see these qualities *fleshed out* before your eyes, in real life. So many of the mentors in scripture displayed the character that made them models for the mentoring process.

WHAT IS SUPPOSED TO HAPPEN IN A MENTORING RELATIONSHIP?

This brings us to the second question we'll address in this chapter. Frequently, I will hear someone say, "I have never been in a formal mentoring relationship with anyone. What exactly is supposed to happen when you meet with a mentor or a mentoree? Is there an optimal format to follow? What sort of exchange should happen?"

The answer to these questions lies in the following pages of this devotional. You are going to be introduced to thirty-two mentoring relationships, which demonstrate what mentoring can and should look like. Each of them are unique in format and context. They reveal there is no one right thing to say or do when you meet with your partner. Some of these biblical mentors met regularly with their mentoree to support them, over an extended period of time. Others simply sized up a situation, gave them some wise counsel and went on their way. What they accomplished varied greatly. However, the one common quality all the good mentors shared is: they modeled what they taught. They didn't just *say it,* they *lived it.* They provided an example for their mentorees to follow.

In addition to this essential ingredient, I've listed below the *God-given resources* that I believe every good mentor should impart to their mentoree, over time. If you are just beginning this process, this list should be especially helpful to you. The following list represents *seven categories* that will provide a guideline, as you think through what "gifts" or resources could and should be exchanged on a regular basis.

SEVEN GIFTS A MENTOR GIVES

Category	Description
1. Accountability	This involves holding a person to their commitments to God. It may involve bringing a list of tough questions to the meeting, and asking them to respond honestly to them.
2. Affirmation	This involves speaking words of encouragement, love and support to your partner; affirming their strengths, their thoughts, their ministry and their obedience.
3. Assessment	This involves evaluating their present state, objectively, and giving them an assessment on what you see; it enables them to gain perspective from an outside viewpoint.

4. Advice.................................. This involves speaking words of wise counsel and giving them options for their decisions. It means providing direction and navigation for their life.

5. Admonishment..................... This involves lending them words of caution and warning to enable them to avoid pitfalls they may not foresee as well as you do. It may mean you provide correction.

6. Assets................................. This involves giving them tangible resources, gifts and resources—whether it's a book, a tape, a ministry tool or a personal contact that you can introduce to them.

7. Application......................... This involves pointing them in the right direction to find places where they can apply truth they've learned; you help them find a "laboratory" where they can practice.

All of these are gifts, given from the heart and life experience of the mentor. They become especially valuable based on the timing in which they are given. I would suggest that you memorize this list, then look for them in the subsequent pages, as you study the mentors and mentorees found in the scripture. My hope is that these relationships provide some wonderful illustrations of this list, that you can reproduce.

THE GREATEST MENTORS IN THE BIBLE

All of this material brings us to the point of this devotional guide. Take some time and determine which level you are on. Are you looking for a mentor? Are you needing to increase your commitment to the mentoring process? Will you answer the call to go deeper with your mentor? Are you ready to reproduce yourself with a mentoree? The purpose of this book is threefold:

1. For the mentor to improve their skills in mentoring

2. For the mentoree to glean from the insight of the greatest mentors in biblical history

*3. For every reader to be mentored long distance as we ob-
serve the match-ups and interaction between mentors and
mentorees in ancient Israel.*

In the pages that follow, you will meet some of the greatest
mentors in the Bible. The pages of scripture contain dozens of relationships where family members, friends, political leaders, religious
teachers and common workers mentored others in their life. These
devotional pages contain snapshots of men and women who en-
gaged in the art of mentoring (during biblical times) and had their
efforts recorded somewhere between Genesis and Revelation. I'm
so glad they were, because we can learn from each of them.
Mentoring may be a buzzword in our world today, but its practice
is not limited to our generation. As I have already mentioned, the
Hebrew culture was a deeply relational culture, where fathers blessed
sons; where tutors trained their students; where tradesmen culti-
vated their apprentices; and where leaders mentored their disciples.

THE CRITERIA...

The criteria for our biblical snapshots is taken from Bobby
Clinton and Paul Stanley's simple definition: *Mentoring is a relational experience where one person empowers another through
the sharing of God-given resources.* Consequently, the three-fold
criteria and objectives for each biblical match-up are:

• Communicating the relational context
• Communicating how they were empowered
• Communicating what the God-given resource was.

Some of you who read through these mentoring snapshots,
will be tempted to do so quickly. No doubt, they are intriguing.
Let me encourage you, however, to slow down and actually study
each of the mentoring match-ups. You may want to examine one a
day or one a week, as a part of your daily devotional study time.
Each devotion includes some key **reflect and respond** sections,
where you can write down what God seems to be teaching you
about mentoring. I trust this study will launch you into the greatest
mentoring match-ups in your life.

ABRAHAM
& LOT

Genesis 12:1-9, 13, 18:22-33

Several years ago, newspapers in my city carried a story I think I'll never forget. It was a story of a crime committed by an arrogant young man named Jason—who also happened to be the son of a wealthy, local business owner. At his trial, he was found guilty of embezzlement, yet even up through the rendering of the verdict, Jason appeared unconcerned, proud and nonchalant. Certainly, he was not humbled or broken by the experience, thus far.

When the verdict was brought in, however, the judge told the defendant to stand for the sentence. He stood, still somewhat cocky and proud. It was at this point that he glanced across the courtroom, only to notice at his attorney's table—his father, too, was standing. His dad had recognized his own involvement with his son's outcome.

Jason looked at his father—who had once walked and stood erect with head and shoulders straight, as those of an honest man with a clear conscience. Now those same shoulders were bowed low with sorrow and shame—as if he were receiving the sentence himself. At the sight of his father, bent and humiliated, Jason finally began to weep bitterly and for the first time repented of his crime. During the years of his prison term, great reform occurred in this young man's life—because of the identification his father felt with him.

It was a powerful story. And it is this same kind of tenacious love and identification that we see in the life of Abraham concerning his nephew, Lot.

Abraham is famous for being the "father of many nations" and the "patriarch of the Jews." However, he was also the uncle of a young man named Lot. These two, along with their families, journeyed together over miles and miles of land, pursuing the territory which God had told Abraham He would give him.

We can surmise that these two men must have been close, as an uncle and nephew often are. From the very call from God to "go forth from your country," Lot was with him. During their time together, Abraham demonstrated the kind of life every mentor ought to live. In fact, there were three specific qualities Abraham exhibited before Lot that we need to give and receive today. Notice these qualities outlined below.

ABRAHAM DEMONSTRATED A SURRENDERED SPIRIT

Lot watched Abraham demonstrate his faith by leaving a comfortable, prosperous home and trade (12:4-6); he observed Abraham build altars to the Lord along the way (12:7); he saw him live with remarkable contentment in strange places, all the while calling on the Lord in his personal prayer times (12:8). If nothing else, Abraham mentored Lot by the model of his lifestyle alone. Genesis 22 is an example. He consistently demonstrated a life that was:

1. *Available to the Plan of God* (v.1-3)
2. *Abandoned to the Purposes of God* (v.4-10)
3. *Assured of the Provision of God* (v.11-14)

ABRAHAM DEMONSTRATED A GENEROUS SPIRIT

There was a second quality. When strife arose from the herdsmen belonging to the two men, Uncle Abraham confronted Lot. After a significant period of time together, Abraham recognized it was time to launch his nephew into new a growth stage (Genesis 13). It was time to separate. Because Abraham wanted no strife between the two families, he offered Lot the opportunity to choose what land he wanted. Naturally, Lot chose the best looking piece of land in sight. The "grass truly was greener" for Lot at this point in his life, as compared to what remained for his uncle. Abraham had consistently demonstrated a true, *generous spirit* to him; he was a model of generosity, as a mentor.

This wasn't the end of the story, however. The good real estate that Lot chose became a thorn for him. Lot ended up in the city of Sodom, where morals were low and loose living was high. The sin was so thick, justice demanded a response. God decided to destroy the area where Lot was living.

ABRAHAM DEMONSTRATED A TENACIOUS SPIRIT

It was at this point that Abraham not only demonstrated further generosity, but also a *tenacious love* and concern for his nephew. Lot had clearly made some wrong decisions. He had slipped into compromise and sin. But his godly uncle began to intercede, and confront his God with a boldness that had yet to be seen in scripture. In Genesis 18, he becomes Lot's advocate or attorney. He knew that God was just, and would not destroy the city if there were even a handful of righteous people. He also trusted that all the mentoring he had given to his nephew had somehow paid off. He assumed that Lot was one of the handful of righteous people in that city. It was this forthright and godly tenacity, optimism and intercession that saved Lot's life, when Sodom was ruined.

Mentoring Keys

THE MENTORING RELATIONSHIP: *Uncle and nephew*

THE METHOD OF EMPOWERMENT: *Time and availability; lifestyle demonstration; tangible gifts (his own possessions)*

THE GOD GIVEN RESOURCES: *A godly model; a generous spirit; intercession; land and livestock*

REFLECT AND RESPOND...

1. What gives a mentor the ability to continue giving to a mentoree, even when the mentoree shows no sign of maturity? (Lot remained selfish and short sighted all his life.)

2. What could Lot have done to become a better mentoree?

3. How does a mentor develop a "generous spirit?"

4. Why do so many fail to become consistent intercessors? How did Abraham seem to overcome those hurdles in his life, as he interceded for Lot? What sort of things might be best to pray for someone you are mentoring?

5. Why do you suppose Lot failed to "glean" more from his mentor? What enables us, today, to gain from our mentors? What makes us "spiritual sponges" that soak up the wisdom and experience of our mentors?

JACOB
&JOSEPH

Genesis 37:1-4, 28-35, 48:11-12

In his book, *The Effective Father,* Gordon MacDonald writes about Boswell, the famous author and biographer of Samuel Johnson. Boswell often referred to a special day in his childhood when his father took him fishing. The day was fixed in his mind, and he frequently reflected on it as a day when his dad had mentored him in an unusual way. It was a watershed day in his maturity, as far as Boswell was concerned. He later wrote about the many things his father taught in the course of their fishing experience together.

After having heard of that particular mentoring excursion so often, it occurred to someone much later to check the journal that Boswell's father kept and determine what had been said on that fishing trip, from the parental perspective. Turning to that date, the reader found only one sentence entered: "Gone fishing today with my son; a day wasted."

I believe we "mentors" often have no idea the impact our words carry. Boswell's father certainly didn't. In his mind, the day was a wash. Yet it had changed the life of his son and mentoree. It reminds me of the admiration that young Joseph had for his father Jacob. No doubt the two had an intimate love for each other—but Jacob likely had no idea of the influence he had in Joseph's life until his son bowed before him in his twilight years.

Few sons experience the kind of favor that Joseph did, from his father Jacob. Although he came from a large family of twelve brothers, young Joseph was set apart by his dad, and given special mentoring, unique gifts and favored status. Some might even argue that it was an unhealthy favoritism, but that is not the point of the argument here. It is our goal to examine the kind of resources that Jacob passed on to his son/mentoree, Joseph.

When we first see Joseph described in detail, he is seventeen years old, and already having dreams from the Lord. No doubt, he was a special young man. Jacob loved him more than all his other sons (Genesis 37:3). He lavished him with gifts, including a highly ornamented coat, which drew the jealousy of his siblings (Genesis 37:3-4). When Joseph had his two dreams which invited the wrath and violence of his brothers, Jacob attempted to bring counsel and correction to him and his attitude (v. 10-11). Right or wrong, Jacob wasn't afraid to speak out for what he believed; and he *spoke into Joseph's life* more than once through his teen years. Although Joseph wasn't the "first born son," Jacob was apparently determined to "bless" him and to insure that he would reach his potential.

Needless to say, when Joseph's brothers beat him and sold him as a slave to the Midianite merchants—Jacob was devastated. The one in whom he had invested so much was now gone. The story he received was that Joseph was dead. Jacob ripped his clothes and wept. His mourning went on for many days (Genesis 37:34). Years of testing occurred for both Jacob (the mentor) and Joseph (the mentoree), while he was in Egypt.

Years later, the mentor and mentoree were reunited. It was a lilting moment when Jacob realized not only that Joseph was still alive, but that he had literally realized his dreams! The two of them kissed and embraced, then exchanged words. Jacob exclaimed, "I never expected to see your face again, and now God has allowed me to see your children, too" (Genesis 48:11).

This was a moving and emotional moment for Joseph. Although he was second in command of Egypt, he still recognized his father as his mentor and spiritual leader. In response to his dad, he removed his children from their grandfather's lap, and bowed down with his face toward to the ground (Genesis 48:12). Their special relationship, and the novelty of their love for each other had not waned. In Genesis 49, when Jacob blesses each of his sons, the longest words of blessing and affirmation are reserved for Joseph. He closes by saying: "Your father's blessings are greater than the blessings of the ancient mountains, than the bounty of the age old hills. Let all these rest on the head of Joseph, on the brow of the prince among his brothers."

Mentoring Keys

The Mentoring Relationship: *Father and Son*

The Method of Empowerment: *Time; favor; gifts; counsel and words of blessing*

The God Given Resources: *Favor/loyalty; wisdom; esteem and affirmation*

Reflect and Respond...

1. Jacob, no doubt, hand picked Joseph for a special mentoring relationship because he was the son of his old age. What factors go into your selection of a mentoree?

2. We all speak different "languages of love." These are commonly described this way:

> 1. *The language of "time spent with a person..."*
> 2. *The language of "words of affirmation..."*
> 3. *The language of "deeds of service..."*
> 4. *The language of "physical touch/affection..."*
> 5. *The language of "tangible gifts..."*

How do you suppose the gifts that Jacob gave to Joseph spoke of his love, favor and loyalty? Do you know how to speak your mentoree's language of love?

3. Why were Jacob's words of "blessing" so important and significant to Joseph? What do the words of a mentor do to a mentoree?

4. Near the end of their story, Joseph maintains his position of submission by bowing before Jacob, his dad and mentor. What enables a mentoree to retain this kind of respect for a mentor?

5. What do you think were the greatest lessons that Joseph learned from his mentor?

Jethro & Moses

Exodus 18:13-27

Dr. Howard Hendricks speaks fondly of the mentors he had in his younger years. He tells of one professor, in particular, who had an impact on his life during his collegian days. Hendricks passed his home many times, early in the morning and late at night, and often saw him pouring over his books. This sight stuck in the mind of the young student. One day, Hendricks asked him, "Doctor, I'd like to know—what is it that keeps you studying? You never cease to learn."

His answer was simple and profound: "Son, I would rather have my students drink from a running stream than from a stagnant pool."

It was this same mindset that prompted Moses to glean from his father-in-law, Jethro. Long after Moses had become the respected commander of the people of Israel, he became the mentoree and student of Jethro. He wasn't too old or too proud to continue learning.

Moses was not a novice at leadership. He had led the children of Israel across the Red Sea and across miles of desert land. He had already been given full permission by God and the people to assume command of the Israeli people, by the middle of the book of Exodus.

It was at this point, however, that he encounters some wrinkles in his system of management. Life had become difficult, his days had become long, and the job had begun to make him weary. Exodus 18:13 states: "...Moses sat to judge the people, and the people stood about Moses from the morning until the evening." He didn't seem to see the obvious. This one man show wasn't fair to him or to the people he attempted to serve! So, what was he supposed to do?

Enter Jethro, his beloved father-in-law—and soon to be mentor. In Exodus 18:13-27 we meet Jethro, a man with a deep concern for the welfare of Moses and the people he was attempting to oversee. Jethro begins to speak timely words into the life of Moses, and he begins with the simple question: "What is this thing you are doing for the people?" and "Why are you doing it alone?" Jethro could vividly see the big picture when Moses failed to do so. Moses' simply responded with, "Because the people come to me..." He was guilty of playing "defense" instead of offense in his leadership. He was being *reactive*, when Jethro began to exhort him to become *proactive*.

In the passage that follows, Jethro became a mentor; a confidant; a counselor; a consultant and a companion for this season of Moses' life. Note the gifts Jethro gives him:

- He warns him of the pitfalls of his present lifestyle (v.17-18).
- He offers wise counsel on the role that Moses should play (v.19-20).
- He provides a plan for delegating the workload to capable helpers (v.21-22).
- He envisions and communicates a "win/win" scenario for Moses and the people (v.23).

In sharing with Moses, Jethro demonstrates a keen intellect that he is willing to share; a deep love for Moses; a discerning spirit when it comes to human nature and endurance; and a submission to God, as he concludes with the words: "If you do this thing and *God so commands you,* then you will be able to endure, and all these people will go to their place in peace." This is the godly mentoring that money just can't buy, but that Moses needed at precisely this time in his career.

It would've have been easy for Jethro to not get involved. After all, Moses was God's chosen leader. Jethro was just a sheepherder from Midian. Further, the problem was gigantic and would require both time and patience to set a plan in motion. What if he was wrong in his advice? What if Moses refused his opinion out of pride, and degraded him?

These were all risks that Jethro, a wise mentor/consultant, was willing to take. He somehow knew that taking initiative was all a part of making investments in Moses' life.

Mentoring Keys

THE MENTORING RELATIONSHIP: *Father-in-law and Son-in-law*

THE METHOD OF EMPOWERMENT: *Initiative; speaking into Moses' life; offering some wise counsel Moses didn't have already*

THE GOD GIVEN RESOURCES: *Time spent; vision and a plan for Moses' career; love and concern for Moses; wisdom and discernment*

REFLECT AND RESPOND...

1. Jethro took initiative with Moses. What keeps you from taking initiative with your mentoree? What must you do to be more willing to take this kind of risk?

2. Jethro spoke into Moses' life in a timely way, and with authority. What does timing have to do with good mentoring?

3. What made Moses a good mentoree? What enables us to be hungry to learn from a mentor? (What qualities would make a mentor want to invest in us?)

4. How do we gain authority in the life of our mentoree?

5. What do you suppose gave Jethro the ability to see the "big picture" of Moses' mistakes, and to develop a plan of action so fitting for the situation? Can we learn from him?

6. What do you suppose were the greatest lessons that Moses learned from his mentor?

Moses
&Joshua

Exodus 33:11, Numbers 27:15-23, Deuteronomy 34:9

Deanna was a high school student who worked and studied hard, and usually achieved excellent grades. She had taken "chemistry" as a college requirement, and had applied herself in all of the assignments—but for some reason, wasn't faring well. It just wasn't her thing. She flunked the course. No doubt, this was a first for Deanna. It would surely devastate her and her family.

Fortunately, her teacher was an unusual man. He had the heart of a mentor and had taken a personal interest in Deanna. He did not feel threatened by her failure, and knew she would go on to flourish as a college student. However, he still had to give her the "F" on her report card and this troubled him. He was a sensitive man, and his only thought was for Deanna and what this grade would mean to her when she took it home. He was torn, but determined to resolve the issue this way. He put an "F" next to "chemistry" on the card, but out in the margin he wrote these words: "We cannot all be chemists—but oh, how we would all love to be Deannas."

What empowering words. Words that contain both grace and truth. Those are the kind that come from rare mentors. They objectively address and assess our flops, fumbles and failures, but encourage and enable us at the same time. All of us need this kind of input during our lifetime, but sadly, many never receive it. Fortunately for a young man named Joshua, this kind of mentor came along for him when he met Moses.

When Joshua took his place as the number one apprentice of Moses, we gain a snapshot of one of the classic mentoring matchups in the Bible. So thorough was the apprenticeship of Joshua, that the only facet Moses neglected was to teach Joshua how to find another "Joshua!" Unfortunately, the mentoring and reproduction seemed to end with him.

Joshua is first introduced as the commander of Moses' Israeli army (Exodus 17). After that point, the two seem to possess a growing relationship, built upon trust and training. Clearly, Joshua was hungry to be mentored, as is demonstrated by his refusal to "leave the tent of Moses" in Exodus 33:11. The following three truths capture the primary "gifts" that Moses gave to Joshua as his leadership mentor.

First, Moses gave Joshua *empowerment*. When God informed Moses that Joshua was to be his understudy, He told Moses to lay hands on him in front of all the people. This event clearly must have been empowering for Joshua, as he was publicly commissioned and even given "part of Moses' authority" (Numbers 27:15-23)! In this process, Joshua received positive recognition; he received his leader's approval and acceptance; and he received Moses' and God's expression of faith in him. No doubt, this was a watershed day for Joshua that he must have recorded in his journal!

Second, Moses gave Joshua *encouragement and affirmation*. He affirmed his young protégé by allowing unusual companionship in some rare places. For instance, when Moses went up on the mountain to hear from God—all the Israelites proceeded to construct a golden calf and worship it as an idol. That is, all except for Joshua—he was with Moses on the mountain. The two of them shared a unique intimacy, particularly when we consider the apparent difference in their ages. They must have made up for the generation gap with a common love for Yahweh and a lot of shared vision for leadership.

Third, Moses gave Joshua *experience*. Joshua's apprenticeship was not merely cerebral and passive; it didn't simply consist of the two of them talking over coffee. It went beyond information from the very beginning. Joshua proved his passion for leadership on the battlefield; he demonstrated his vision for leadership when he and Caleb returned from spying out the land with a "good report" full of faith. Consequently, Moses lavished upon him confidence and trust. He also gave Joshua knowledge and insight regarding national affairs and problems, as well. Further, Moses shared the public recognition in successes, as he praised his mentoree before the people on more than one occasion.

Mentoring Keys

THE MENTORING RELATIONSHIP: *National Leader and Apprentice*

THE METHOD OF EMPOWERMENT: *Shared events; on the job training; affirmation; trust; intimate companionship; life modeling*

THE GOD GIVEN RESOURCES: *Experience; confidence and recognition; wisdom and authority*

REFLECT AND RESPOND...

1. Moses trusted Joshua, as a capable apprentice. What effect does this have on a mentoree, when trust is given?

2. What made Joshua such a "model" mentoree? What can we duplicate from his life as an apprentice under Moses?

3. Joshua had the privilege of sharing in some one-of-a-kind experiences with Moses. How is this an even better way of mentoring, than simple discussion?

4. What did Joshua gain from the shared experiences with his mentor? How might this help us to approach the right mentor for our lives? How might it help us in the *method* in which we approach our mentor?

5. Moses accomplished something extremely valuable for Joshua when he publicly gave him affirmation and authority, during his commissioning. How might you accomplish this same thing today?

DEBORAH & BARAK

Judges 4:4-16

Every year, families converge in Colorado for some natural, rugged, adventuresome mountain climbing experiences. The Rockies are famous for providing a perfect environment for amateurs to scale the sides of some of the most beautiful terrain anywhere in the U.S.

One such family decided to take a risk, and climb a rock that was steeper than any they'd ever attempted before. Together they determined that dad should go first, and be the forerunner for the rest of them. Slowly, he began to inch his way upward, cautiously choosing each step, making sure it was secure enough to hold his weight, and that of the rest of his clan. After progressing about 100 feet, his son began to climb. His progress was quite a bit faster than dad's, since he was able to take advantage of the path created by his "forerunner." It was an exercise in trust. Somewhere midway up the mountain, the boy exhorted his dad with words that every mentor needs to hear from their mentorees. He simply said: "Choose your route carefully, dad. We're all following right behind you, taking every step you do."

For some, that statement could sound frightening. Who in their right mind wants that kind of responsibility? On the other hand, what a privilege to know that significant people in our life would intentionally follow in our footsteps! All of us need "forerunners" not just on a mountain, but in life—who can model which paths to choose as we walk through our own journeys. Barak felt this need, when he chose a woman named Deborah to be his mentor.

In Judges 4 we are introduced to Deborah, the only woman in the distinguished company of Israel's judges.

She became a judge (national leader) and mentor to Barak, a military leader, at a time of crisis. The plight of the northern tribes was clearly known to her and, conversely, they were not only aware of her reputation but came to her with their request for help, in their predicament (v.5). Israel was under siege by the King of Canaan. At the time of crisis, Deborah was already established as a prophetess and judge in the non-military sphere. It was her demonstration of charismatic qualities in this realm that led the tribes to seek her assistance. It was at this point, that she summons and challenges Barak in the name of Yahweh—to lead Israel's army. She is direct. She is affirming. She gives clear marching orders, in great detail. I am certain that this took place over hours of conversation, since Barak was particularly hesitant to take on such a challenge. She mentored him on his path to success. She spoke into his life and committed to join him in his plight—until he was convinced that he ought to take the risk and obey.

The lack of courage Barak displays is understandable, humanly speaking. The disparity between Israel's forces and the opposition was formidable. He convinced Deborah that he needed a mentor by his side through the process. He made her presence the condition of his acceptance. In her acceptance, there is a hint of displeasure at his attitude as she announced that the need of a woman would eclipse any honor due him (v.9). As it turned out, this didn't seem to bother Barak. They went out together, with an army of 10,000 and defeated Canaan. Deborah and Barak serve as a rare illustration in the Bible of a successful relationship, where a female mentored a male.

Because of this unusual relationship, these two individuals give us a glimpse of the absolute essentials, for a mentoring match-up. The following list reveals the necessary ingredients (the bare minimum) for both mentors and for mentorees today:

ESSENTIALS FOR THE MENTOREE...

1. *Relationship with the mentor.* Deep impact requires relationship between the mentor and mentoree. While information can be transmitted in a sterile "classroom," mentoring is a much more

personal process. It often increases in impact as the intimacy deepens.

2. Respect for the mentor. A mentoree must possess a level of respect for the mentor, if he/she is going to learn from them. Barak certainly demonstrates this (as do the rest of the Israelites) when he not only relies on Deborah but requests her presence in his assignment.

ESSENTIALS FOR THE MENTOR...

1. Responsive to the mentoree. When a mentor chooses an apprentice, good "chemistry" between the two should be a major factor. The mentor must determine: who they like, who they feel they can help, who they are open to spend time with, who they believe in.

2. Resources for the mentoree. The mentor must discern that they have something to offer the mentoree. I believe Deborah chose Barak not only because she believed in him, but because she could lend him insight and direction for the task at hand. She had gifts he needed.

The primary negative component to Deborah and Barak's mentoring relationship was simply this: he had an inordinate need for *reliance upon his mentor.* He felt he couldn't "do it without her." This kind of dependency is fine for the beginner, but like a child who must be weaned from their parents—so the mentoree must take the resources offered by the mentor, and move forward in their challenges, on their own.

Mentoring Keys

THE MENTORING RELATIONSHIP: *Judge and Military Leader*

THE METHOD OF EMPOWERMENT: *Affirmation; belief in him; clear direction; her personal time and availability*

THE GOD GIVEN RESOURCES: *Wisdom; military strategy; her personal presence and support; authority.*

REFLECT AND RESPOND...

1. Clearly, Deborah and Barak were a rare mentoring match up. The Hebrew culture made it difficult for a man to receive from a woman. Why do you suppose Barak was so drawn to Deborah, and had no problem requesting her help?

2. What unique qualities and gifts have you noticed that women have to offer mentorees?

3. Do you have both males and females that speak into your life? Can you receive input and perspective from both genders? Why or why not?

4. Deborah joined Barak in his assigned task. Have you ever requested such help? What are the positives and negatives of such a dependency on a mentor?

Naomi
& Ruth

Ruth 1:1-22, 3:1-5, 4:13-17

A woman who taught first graders in a Texas panhandle school decided one day that it just wasn't worth it anymore. She drew this conclusion after an especially draining day at her elementary school. She wrote in her journal:

"I just attended an incredibly long PTA meeting. My 30 first graders squirmed restlessly all day long today. The reading groups actually seemed to be moving backward; recess was hot, windy and gritty; at four o'clock Mrs. Jones burst into my classroom weeping because her Jenny was not in the top reading group anymore; I forgot to turn in an important report to the principle—and to top it all off, I snagged my nylons just after the last bell rang."

She determined to quit teaching that day, as she drove to the university where she was finishing up her master's degree. She knew there had to be more to life than teaching kids. "I'll grow a garden. I'll write a book. But I won't teach school," she said to herself as she slumped into her seat at the university. She didn't even bother listening to the professor; after all, what's the use? I won't be going back! But she was wrong. Again, in her own words, she wrote in her diary:

The friendly woman who sat next to me in my masters class leaned over and said, "I saw an admirer of yours yesterday." She paused, as I sat up in my seat. "Oh?" I began to listen with growing interest. "I met a young girl and her mother at the bus station who would soon be moving to Colorado to join her father," she continued. "We spoke for a while, then she took a photograph from her pocket—but it wasn't of her father or another family member she would soon see. I was astonished to see it was a picture of *you.* 'This is the person I will miss the most. This is the teacher I really love,' the young girl said. When I mentioned that I knew you, she beamed with joy and acted like she wanted to kiss me. You are sort of a celebrity to her!"

This conversation caused that first grade teacher to go home and do some deep soul searching. She kept reflecting on the words of that young girl she didn't even know: "This is the person I will miss the most. This is the teacher I really love." All of a sudden, it struck her that she didn't teach "first grade"—she taught people! Real, live children who are impressionable were watching her every move. Immediately, she couldn't think of anything she would rather do.

The feelings expressed by the six year old girl must have been the ones felt by Ruth, in the Old Testament as she pondered moving away from her mother-in-law, Naomi. She wanted to stay with her; this woman was the mentor that she "really loved." At the same time, Naomi must have determined that it would be better to invest herself in the "living" than to squander time dwelling on her family who had passed away.

Like the first grade girl, Ruth couldn't imagine life without her teacher, Naomi. As it turned out, Naomi welcomed her request to remain with her, and the two began a journey as mentor and mentoree. At least as far as this study guide goes, Naomi and Ruth are the first two females who deliberately match up, for the purpose of mentoring. Early in the book, both women lose their husbands, and Naomi encourages Ruth to go back to her homeland to find another. But Ruth refuses to leave her, despite no blood ties or obligations. Ruth simply wants to be around this godly mentor and learn from her (Ruth 1:14-16).

The basis for their positive experience with mentoring was pure *relationship.* This is true for all good mentoring match-ups, but is particularly true for females. Love, trust and understanding were the framework for these two women from two different generations. Both had experienced tremendous pain in their adults lives, having been widowed. Ruth must have respected Naomi's ability to deal with her loss when she lost her own husband. I say this, because Ruth completely transferred her allegiance to Naomi, including the sharing of her culture and her faith! (Ruth wasn't a Hebrew, she was from Moab!)

Naomi has words of wise counsel for young Ruth from the very beginning. Naomi chose Bethlehem as their settling place, and her mentoree completely trusted her judgment. She must have believed that Naomi had her best interests in mind, because Ruth does not ever bring up "catching another man" as they make their decisions. In fact, it is Naomi who sees the potential relationship with Boaz emerge, and she gives her helpful direction as that relationship surfaces (Ruth 3:1-5). Ruth performs everything Naomi tells her to do.

Although we might be tempted to stereotype Naomi into the comedic image of a Jewish mother-in-law (however untrue that image is), we never get the impression that Naomi is controlling or condescending in her mentoring of Ruth. Clearly, Naomi can see the needs that Ruth will have in the future, and she addresses them, directly and in a healthy manner. By the end of their story, Naomi is rewarded by Ruth giving birth to a son. The pleasure that came from that surrogate grandmother role must have sustained her in her twilight years, that might have otherwise been lonely for her as a widow. She got to be the nurse of Ruth and Boaz's baby boy. We see a happy mentor and a fulfilled mentoree by the close of the book, in Ruth 4:13-17.

Mentoring Keys

THE MENTORING RELATIONSHIP: *Mother-in-law and Daughter-in-law*

THE METHOD OF EMPOWERMENT: *Availability; godly counsel; empathy*

THE GOD GIVEN RESOURCES: *Wisdom and companionship*

REFLECT AND RESPOND...

1. At the close of chapter one, Naomi is embittered because she has been widowed. She had no husband and no sons to carry on the family name. Yet, Ruth recognizes the value in sticking with her, as a mentor. What do you suppose Ruth saw in Naomi that made her want to remain with her? How can mentorees spot valuable mentors?

2. What needs did Ruth meet in Naomi's life, once they returned to Bethlehem? In what ways was it therapeutic for Naomi to mentor that young woman?

3. Why was Naomi in an especially good position to mentor Ruth? How might the answer to this question help us today in selecting a mentor/mentoree match-up?

4. How can mentors demonstrate that they have the best interests of their mentorees in mind? How did Naomi do it with Ruth?

5. What made Ruth such a great mentoree?

Nehemiah
& His Kinsmen

Nehemiah 3, 5

Little Tyler was in the second grade, when his teacher gave the class a sizable homework assignment. Tyler began to fret and become a little put out with his teacher. Finally he asked skeptically, "Do you get paid for teaching us?"

The teacher smiled. "Yes."

Puzzled, the boy exclaimed, "That's funny! We do all the work!"

I suppose it is possible that the men who submitted themselves to Nehemiah, as their leader and mentor might have felt the same way. Nehemiah was a master motivator. His book tells the story of a man who became the mentor of his kinsmen, and mobilized them to build a wall around the city of Jerusalem, in record time: fifty two days! He was able to do this, not because he was a task master or a driven tyrant or a crusty boss—but because he understood *people* and how to motivate them. Chapters two through five record how he moved a bunch of "volunteers" to perform a task that few thought could ever be pulled off in their lifetime.

This leader would be called a "mentor-coach" by Dr. Robert Clinton. He was a mentor who enabled mentorees to perform a job that they couldn't seem to pull off without his help. He wasn't simply their cheerleader, either. He organized the workers into groups and implemented a strategy through them. He proved the principle that: *motivation without organization leads to frustration.* Notice the principles he employed to empower his mentorees, found in chapter three alone:

THE PRINCIPLE OF SIMPLIFICATION
He organized the men around natural groupings: their fami-

lies, (v.1). He imposed no unnecessary organizational "red tape." He demonstrated that lots of prayer, planning and preparation causes the work to come off smooth and simple. No one fully knew the volume of preparation Nehemiah put in to empowering these mentorees.

THE PRINCIPLE OF PARTICIPATION

In verses 2-10 we read the words: "next to them..." Nehemiah found a way to get much accomplished by moving with those who wanted to move in his direction. Lots of folks were involved because he was able to spot those who wanted to *do something!* We learn in verse 5 that we're to *love everyone*—but *move with the movers* when they are ready.

THE PRINCIPLE OF DELEGATION

Next, we see a beautiful picture of delegation, as Nehemiah gave specific assignments to fitting people. He matched tasks with men. He divided the project up into 42 groups and 13 sections, breaking down the goals into actual jobs. This is how to insure that delegation works: reduce the big picture into bite size tasks that are clear and measurable.

THE PRINCIPLE OF MOTIVATION

At this point, the mentor Nehemiah allows for ownership on the part of his mentorees. In verses 10, 23, 28-30 we observe how he did it: he motivated people to do their best by allowing them to work on the wall that was in front of their own house! Talk about incentive—everyone was at peak performance having something at stake in the job.

THE PRINCIPLE OF COOPERATION

Further, this mentor encouraged *teamwork*, not just involvement. There's something about being a part of a work that is bigger than any could pull off as individuals. The word commonly used to describe this phenomena is: synergy. It represents the exponential force that is harnessed by putting our heads, hands and hearts together toward one goal.

THE PRINCIPLE OF AFFIRMATION

Finally, Nehemiah knew the power of expressing apprecia-tion and recognition. He knew all of their names, and saw them all at work, including the daughters, which are listed in verse 12. This was unique in hebrew culture. The mentor affirmed them, and ex-pressed his gratitude to them for their effort.

This mentor teaches us much regarding the accomplishment of a task through people. There is so much untapped potential in the Body of Christ today, because leaders do not know how to em-power followers (or mentorees). Consequently, the mentor, the mentoree and the Body all lose, in the end.

Mentoring Keys

THE MENTORING RELATIONSHIP: *A Leader and His Kinsmen(common ethnic affinity)*

THE METHOD OF EMPOWERMENT: *Initiative; implemen-tation of strategy and lots of motivation! (See prin-ciples listed above)*

THE GOD GIVEN RESOURCES: *An opportunity to suc-ceed; increased morale and esteem; restored pride in themselves & their abilities*

REFLECT AND RESPOND...

1. Nehemiah accomplished this record breaking feat, despite the lack of any special authority among his own people. How do we gain authority and influence in someone's life when it isn't given to us, naturally, by a position?

2. Most mentors today are simply sources of wisdom and insight for mentorees. Nehemiah was able to accomplish some major work through his mentorees. Make a list of what you see that the mentorees (or workers) both *gave* and *gained* by submitting to Nehemiah.

3. Do you have a "mentor-coach" who guides you in your work? How is this different than simply a mentor who gives counsel? Are you a mentor-coach for anyone, yourself?

4. What is the most significant lesson you learn from this mentoring encounter?

MORDECAI & ESTHER

Esther 2:1-11, 4:1-14

Many boys can remember days during their childhood when they watched their dad model a principle that somehow changed their life. Dan Clark, contributor to *Chicken Soup for the Soul,* (Volume Two) recalls one particular day with his dad:

Once when I was a teenager, my father and I were standing in line to buy tickets for the circus. Finally, there was only one family between us and the ticket counter. This family made a big impression on me. There were eight children, all probably under the age of twelve. You could tell they didn't have a lot of money. Their clothes were not expensive but they were clean. The children were well-behaved, all of them standing in line, two by two behind their parents holding hands. They were excitedly jabbering about the clowns, elephants and other acts they were about to see. One could sense they had never been to the circus before. It promised to be the highlight of their young lives.

The father and mother were at the head of the pack standing as proud as could be...when the ticket lady asked the man how many tickets he wanted. He proudly responded, "Please, let me buy eight children's tickets and two adult tickets so I can take my family to the circus."

The ticket lady quoted the price.

The man's wife let go of his hand, her head dropped; the man's lip began to quiver. He leaned a little closer and asked, "How much did you say?"

The ticket lady again quoted the price. The man didn't have enough money—but how was he supposed to turn and tell his eight kids that he didn't have enough money to take them to the circus?

Seeing what was going on, my dad put his hand into his pocket, pulled out a $20 bill and dropped it on the ground. My father reached down, picked up the bill, tapped the man on the shoulder and said, "Excuse me, sir, this fell out of your pocket."

He looked straight into my dad's eyes...and with his lip quivering and a tear streaming down his cheek, he replied, "Thank you, thank you, sir. This really means a lot to my family."

My father and I went back to our car and drove home. We didn't go to the circus that night, but we didn't go without.

Those kind of moments linger in the mind of a son or daughter. They scream of the character and generosity residing in a man's heart. They also help to earn the privilege of speaking into the life of that son or daughter later on. The example has been set.

I can only speculate, but I believe Esther watched Mordecai set such an example as she grew up under his care. He modeled convictions she would later emulate, as an adult. Few stories in the Bible contain all of the drama, romance, suspense and irony that the story of Esther does. It could be described with any of the words above, but it also is a beautiful tale of a mentoring relationship between Mordecai and Queen Esther.

Mordecai was a cousin of Esther. He was much older than the "daughter of his uncle" and when her parents died, he raised her as though she was his own daughter (Esther 2:7). This is significant, because in those early, formative years of her life, Mordecai earned the right to speak very boldly to her as an adult. When she became queen, due to her outward beauty, Mordecai had already invested much into her *inward* beauty. Consequently, her character was strong enough to handle such a visible and influential position. His concern for her continues on into her adult life. As an indicator of his loving, nurturing mentor relationship, and his deep concern for her welfare, he paces out front of her living quarters, when she is in competition for the office of queen (Esther 2:11). Evidently, Mordecai possessed such acute authority in her life that she literally did everything that he instructed her to do. She trusted all of his words of direction and counsel (Esther 2:20).

It is in chapter four that their story reaches its climax, at least from a mentoring standpoint. Mordecai has communicated the details of Haman's plot to slaughter the Hebrew people—both he and Esther are among the Jewish race. Esther balks at his suggestion that she might be a key player in thwarting the plan. After all, she reminds him, she would be risking her life by approaching the king about this issue if she has not been summoned first. Mordecai doesn't bite. He won't have her acting on her fears. His response is a classic case study of how a mentor can "speak into the life" of his mentoree. He spoke to Esther in a timely way; he spoke deeply personal words to her, that called upon her "higher self." He planted in her a sense of destiny, concerning her calling in life.

In chapter four, verses 13-14, he communicates four principles regarding Esther's choice to step out and take a risk, or to play it safe the rest of her life. He issues a challenge, that can be summarized this way: If Esther refused to step out and obey...

1) ...Her fate would not differ from the rest of the crowd (v.13)
2) ...God would find someone else to fulfill His plan (v.14a)
3) ...She might lose more than an opportunity (v.14b)
4) ...She could miss out on fulfilling her life mission (v.14c)

It just might be true that no one else could have spoken so bluntly and forthrightly to her. Esther was the queen. She didn't have to do anything she was told. She had a mentor, however, that would not let her drift into the waters of apathy or mediocrity. He called upon her deepest convictions and spoke into her life "for such a time as this." From Mordecai's investment in her life, she gained a sense of "destiny" and began to understand what her contribution to her world was to be. It became Esther's finest hour.

Mentoring Keys

THE MENTORING RELATIONSHIP: *Cousins (Esther was the younger cousin; the daughter of Mordecai's uncle).*

Mentoring Keys continued...

THE METHOD OF EMPOWERMENT: *Time and a father's heart; deep concern; challenge and confrontation; nurture.*

THE GOD GIVEN RESOURCES: *Future vision; sense of destiny; confidence; direction and perspective.*

REFLECT AND RESPOND...

1. Mordecai had developed a "father's heart" for Esther, by the time she became queen. He had raised her from her childhood. What can we do to develop this kind of heart for people?

2. Esther seemed to follow every word of counsel and direction from Mordecai. What does this reveal to us about Esther's character? About Mordecai's character?

3. Esther received clear words of vision for her future and even gained a "sense of destiny" from Mordecai. Do you have anyone who does this for you? Do you do it for anyone, yourself?

4. What specific steps of preparation did Mordecai take that allowed him to have the right authority to speak to (mentor) her so boldly?

ELI
& SAMUEL

I Samuel 3:1-10

Bennet Cerf relays the touching story about a bus trip that took place in the South, years ago. In one seat was a wispy old man, holding a bunch of fresh flowers. Across the aisle was a young girl whose eyes kept wandering over to those flowers, again and again. The time came for the old man to get off the bus. Impulsively, he thrust the flowers into the girl's lap. "I can see you love flowers," he explained, "and I think my wife would like for you to have them. I'll tell her I gave them to you." The young girl felt awkward, but accepted the flowers—then watched the old man get off the bus and walk through the gate of a small cemetery.

What a difficult but beautiful decision the old man made that day. He somehow figured it was better to invest the flowers into someone who was living and could benefit from them, than to simply honor his wife, who had long since passed away.

In one sense, that was the predicament that Eli found himself in, during his days as a priest. He had two sons, whom he had failed to mentor well. In fact, they became his downfall. They all died dishonorably, but not before Eli took the opportunity to invest in a young boy named Samuel. Young Samuel became the apprentice to Eli, and benefited from the last bunch of "spiritual flowers" the priest had to give.

Samuel was taken to his mentor, by his mother, at a very young age. This may sound strange, but she was keeping a promise. Hannah had been barren for years, and had told God that if He gave her a son, she would allow him to become a priest when he was old enough. Consequently, she had to give him up early, to Eli (the current priest) for the proper training. Hence, Eli became the mentor, by default, for young Samuel. He tutored Samuel as an apprentice in the priestly vocation.

One of the few and early episodes in their mentoring experience came shortly after young Sam had arrived to stay with Eli. While asleep one night, Samuel heard God speaking to him. This was a new experience for him, but one he would learn from, and repeat many times in his ministry.

It is at this point that we begin to observe the imperfections of his mentor. When Eli hears Samuel inquire about the "voice" he hears, Eli doesn't recognize it as God's voice, any faster than Samuel does. He essentially tells him to go back to sleep! The same thing happens a second time. It is only after misinterpreting the voice twice that Eli realizes it must be the Lord. This lack of discernment is symptomatic of Eli's lifestyle. In the next several verses, the scripture communicates how Eli had failed on a much larger scale at raising his sons. It is a sad commentary of how a man can succeed in his workplace, but fail in his home. The good news is this. It appears that Yahweh is indeed a God of second chances—just like the book of Jonah teaches us. Although Eli had failed miserably at mentoring his sons, God gave him a shot at mentoring the priest who would succeed him.

Apparently, God uses imperfect mentors. Imagine that! In the midst of his failures and misinterpretations—God uses Eli to mentor Samuel, and prepare him to be one of Israel's greatest priests. In fact, once he understood what was going on that evening (in chapter three), he helps to posture Samuel to hear God's voice as a lifestyle. He fosters young Samuel toward a place of consistent listening. Samuel began to assume:

1. *Proper Practice* (He was doing God's work) v.1
2. *Proper Proximity* (He was in God's presence, the Temple) v.3
3. *Proper Position* (He was quiet and still before God) v.3

Clearly, this has to encourage us, both as mentorees and potential mentors. Despite his failures, God commissioned Eli to mentor Samuel, and prepare him to do the number one task of a priest: to hear God's voice. The mentoring of Samuel became Eli's greatest feat. In addition, we should note the teachability of Samuel, as a mentoree. He remained completely moldable in the hands of his mentor, and respected his mentor, even when he must have heard negative reports about his personal life. In a sense, he "ate the fish and spit out the bones," embracing all of the helpful resources Eli had to offer, while discarding those unhealthy qualities he neither needed or wanted. He didn't allow the imperfections of his mentor to ruin any of the positive resources he could gain from him.

Mentoring Keys

THE MENTORING RELATIONSHIP: *Priest and Apprentice*

THE METHOD OF EMPOWERMENT: *Vocational tutoring; modeling; words of direction*

THE GOD GIVEN RESOURCES: *Wisdom/teaching; ministry experience through discipleship*

REFLECT AND RESPOND...

1. As we discovered earlier, Eli was *not* a perfect mentor. What do you perceive to be his most significant failures (I Samuel 3-4)? Fortunately, God chose to use him anyway. Write down how this specifically encourages you in the mentoring process.

2. Eli mentored Samuel in his career/vocation. They both had chosen the same profession. Do you have a vocational mentor? A vocational mentoree? What unique mentoring opportunities await this kind of relationship? Be specific.

3. After his apprenticeship with Eli, Samuel becomes a greater priest than his mentor. How would you respond if your mentoree outperformed you?

4. Samuel learned how to hear God's voice from Eli. What's the greatest lesson you have learned from your mentor(s)?

5. What's the most important truth you've learned from this relationship?

JONATHAN & DAVID

I Samuel 18:1, 20:1-42

Next Autumn, when you see geese flying south for the winter, flying along in a "V" formation, you might be interested to know what science has discovered about their flight patterns.

It has been learned that as each bird flaps its wings, it creates an uplift for the bird immediately following. By flying in a "V" formation, the whole flock adds at least 72% flying range than if each bird flew on its own. Whenever a goose falls out of formation, it suddenly feels the drag and resistance of trying to go it alone, and quickly gets into formation to take advantage of the lifting power of the bird directly in front.

When the lead goose gets tired, he rotates back in the wind and another goose flies point. The rest of the geese honk from behind to encourage those up front to keep up their speed and momentum.

Finally, when a goose gets sick, or is wounded by gun shots and falls out, two geese fall out of formation and follow him down to help and protect him. They stay with him until he is either able to fly or until he is dead. They then launch out on their own with another formation to catch up with the group.

Interesting. Not only do these behaviors serve as a model for us as Christians, but they also remind us of the illustration given to us by David and Jonathan, in the Old Testament. The relationship that developed between Jonathan and David is a classic tale of friendship. The two of them began to love each other in a way that very few of us have the privilege of experiencing today. Friendships like this one just don't come along quickly or easily.

I believe, however, it was much more than a friendship that grew between these two young men. I believe Jonathan became a strategic person in David's development because of the deposits he made in both his mind and heart. Call him a "peer mentor" if you will; a "Barnabas" who seems to come along and encourage his colleagues—but I'm convinced from the biblical text that Jonathan made the most significant investment in the forming of David's adult life.

We first read of their relationship in I Samuel 18:1. The text informs us that Jonathan "loved David as he loved himself" and that the soul of Jonathan was "knit to the soul of David." Both began to grow in their trust of one another, until either would do anything for the other. We see this demonstrated in I Samuel 20. David had already slain Goliath, but he was still an understudy when it came to the monarchy. He was a musician in the palace, while Jonathan was the prince; the one in line to succeed his father as king of Israel. It is clear that Jonathan was more concerned with helping David prepare for that role than he was at securing it for himself. If nothing else, Jonathan was selfless and generous.

In chapter 20, David approaches his friend/mentor and informs him of King Saul's desire to take his life. Jonathan cannot believe that his father would want to take the life of David. He is certain that he would've been informed of such a plan. In this single chapter, however, four visible "gifts" are given to David by his mentor, Jonathan. As the two of them converse, these four begin to emerge:

1) AVAILABILITY (v.1-4) In the midst of his disbelief over the news, Jonathan tells David that he is at his disposal. He commits to do whatever David needs to secure his safety and welfare. After all, this is the future King of Israel.

2) DEPENDABILITY (v.5-23) Out of love Jonathan initiates a covenant, complete with a vow to be taken by both of them, to insure David's peace of mind. Accountability is established between the two on a formal basis, and they exchange oaths of commitment. Jonathan has little to gain from this oath personally. He does it for the gain of David.

3) VULNERABILITY (v.24-34) At this point, Jonathan becomes

completely vulnerable, on behalf of David. He shows up at the dinner table with his father; David is missing. When the truth comes out that Saul wants to assassinate David, Jonathan protects David, even while Saul curses him, and then makes an attempt on his life! Jonathan has now declared his priorities. He risks his life for the future of his mentoree.

4) RESPONSIBILITY (v.35-42) When the story is all told, Jonathan communicates to David that his life is in danger, and he implores him to leave. Even when it means losing the best friend he'd ever had, he commits to doing what is right. He bids farewell to his mentoree, in tears. Interestingly, verse 41 tells us that David wept even more. He was losing the greatest encourager and support he'd ever known.

One last footnote. Jonathan must have succeeded in the task of a mentor. Early in their journey together, the scripture tells us that "Jonathan encouraged David" (I Samuel 23:16). Later, after David is thrust out into the cruel world without his mentor, Jonathan—the scripture tells us that "David encouraged himself" (I Samuel 30:6). A good mentor always invests in a mentoree until the mentoree can do it without him.

Mentoring Keys

THE MENTORING RELATIONSHIP: *Best friends (Jonathan is the prince; David is the palace musician)*

THE METHOD OF EMPOWERMENT: *Trust; availability; faith in David; friendship; encouragement and advocacy*

THE GOD GIVEN RESOURCES: *Confidence; protection; esteem; love and support*

REFLECT AND RESPOND...

1. Based upon what you know of Jonathan and David, what do you think attracted these two friends to each other? What factors attract you to a mentor or mentoree?

2. Both of these men took risks for each other during their lives. What kind of ingredients must be involved in a relationship before you'll risk your life for someone?

3. Jonathan built David's self esteem and enabled him to "encourage himself" later in life, rather than depend on someone to encourage him. How do you build esteem in your mentoree? How do you enable them to go beyond relying on your support?

4. How did Jonathan demonstrate loyalty to David?

5. What is the greatest lesson you've drawn from this relationship?

DAVID
& HIS MEN
I Samuel 22:1-2, I Chronicles 11:15-19

Some of the greatest truths about life are taught by those who don't even consider themselves to be teachers. This is certainly true about Dr. Nathaniel Bowditch.

Nathaniel Bowditch, at the age of 21, was captain of a ship that sailed on an East Indian voyage. In route, he determined to take the pains to instruct every member of the crew in the art of navigation. No doubt, it meant late nights, long explanations to those who were a bit slow to pick it up, and repetitive discussions regarding the equipment. However, he knew the value of thorough training: good decisions, healthy camaraderie and deep loyalty.

As a result, every single sailor on board that ship later became a captain of their own ship. Obviously, this is a rare occurrence. Yet it is the kind of outcome that happens when a man is committed to both *training* and *relationship* with those under his care. It is this kind of mentoring that we read about in scripture time and again, particularly from the life of David when he became a military commander in the hills of Judah.

A fascinating story of leadership is recorded from David's life, even before he became King of Israel. In I Samuel 22:1-2, we read how he had to run from Saul, who was determined to assassinate him, out of sheer jealousy. David took refuge in the cave of Adullam, where he was joined by several family members and a rag tag group of men, who decided they wanted to follow him.

Interestingly, David doesn't appear to have been *searching* for mentorees when this group of four hundred people show up. They are somehow attracted to this mentor, being at similar places in their journey: distressed, discontented and in debt (I Samuel 22:2). David must have stayed there a considerable time, and took this brave, reckless crew of potential fighters and built them into a sort of SWAT team; guerrilla warriors, if you will. David even placed his parents in the care of the king of Moab, so that he could await God's direction (v.3-4), and give his attention to the training and mentoring of these men. According to several commentaries, these warriors began to ripen into heroic men under David's tutelage and command. He successfully made "deposits" into their lives, during this time.

I Chronicles 11:15-19 relays a moving story of the dividends paid to a mentor who invests so much in his mentorees. After David had taught them all he knew, he divided them into troops, with "chief men" over the divisions. Three of his chief men were with him one hot day when David's tongue became dry. He was thirsty. He nonchalantly described his memory of the cool water that came from the well at Bethlehem. I'm sure he smiled, as he remembered it. No further words were necessary. Before he could stop them, these three men darted out to retrieve *this water* for their mentor. They could have gotten *any* water to quench his thirst—but they determined to go to the exact well David had described—which happened to be precisely where the enemy troops were stationed! They exhibited absolute loyalty to David, and risked their lives to respond to this small request by him.

What moves a mentoree to demonstrate such loyalty? Volumes could be written in answer to this question, but we must begin by noting one fundamental "people principle:" *People do what people see.* Likely, it wasn't David's sermons or motivating speeches that moved these mentorees. I believe it was watching him model *loyalty,* himself. As I discussed earlier in this book, David embraced the qualities of a good mentor: Godliness, Objectivity, Authenticity, Loyalty and Servanthood. (These spell the word "GOALS".) In return, mentorees often reciprocate such qualities. David reaped the benefits he himself had demonstrated to them. He had modeled this kind of risk taking, faithfulness and courage from the days he fought Goliath, as a teenager. Now he was doing it in a mentoring relationship with a team of "giant slayers." No doubt, the deepest commitments and commradary between men are developed in a "foxhole" or in the fields of battle. If this is true, then

David was in a wonderful laboratory for soliciting such commitment. In his military strategy, and in his respect for Saul (in refus-
ing to take his life) David drew this same kind of attitude (and
respect for authority) from those he led. All of this provided *preparation* for this mentor to lead an entire nation, in the years to come.

Mentoring Keys

THE MENTORING RELATIONSHIP: *Military Commander
and Rebels (renegades)*

THE METHOD OF EMPOWERMENT: *Time; attention;
training; demonstration of tactics; commitment to his
men and support (loyalty)*

THE GOD GIVEN RESOURCES: *Military savvy and skills;
a cause; and a lifestyle*

REFLECT AND RESPOND...

1. When David met up with these mentorees in the cave at Adullam,
we have no evidence that he was looking for people to train. In
your own words, what do you suppose attracted these men to David,
as a mentor? What would attract someone to you?

2. Galatians 6:7 teaches that "whatever a man sows, that will he
also reap." How was this true for David, as he mentored these
men? In what specific ways was he able to gain the loyalty that he
did from the three chief men? How might we do it, today?

3. The qualities that make a good mentoree spell the word FAITH:

F-Faithful
A-Available
I-Initiative
T-Teachable
H-Hungry

How did David's mentorees exhibit that they were ideal mentorees, with these qualities?

4. When David received the water from the Bethlehem well, he refused to drink it, out of respect for the men who obtained it. They had risked their lives. How can we exhibit our appreciation for a mentor/mentoree who demonstrates such loyalty to us?

5. How can we display loyalty and commitment to our mentors or mentorees, today?

DAVID & MEPHIBOSHETH

II Samuel 9:1-13

Most of us are familiar with the biography of Helen Keller. Hers is a moving story of a deaf and blind girl who would have grown up to simply be a "vegetable" if it weren't for a women named Anne Sullivan. Anne entered her life early on, and began to work with Helen on her vocabulary, personal habits, perception/ recognition, manners and speech. By the time Helen reached adulthood, she was a changed woman. When the two of them met, young Helen was in a cage, and would only growl at her new mentor. At the conclusion of Anne's work, Helen was communicating efficiently, eating by herself and taking care of her own personal needs. Anne Sullivan had brought about an absolute revolution in Helen Keller, and helped to build a self-sufficient woman.

This wasn't the end of the story, however. In the later years of her life, Anne Sullivan had a relapse of her previous condition. She became physically ill, and went blind. Ironically, now the "mentor" was in need of someone to work with her. Can you guess who stepped forward to fill the role? It was Helen Keller. She returned the favor; she was able to give back to the one who had given so much to her.

In many ways, this account resembles the situation King David found himself in, after his mentor, Jonathan passed away. Although he wasn't able to give back to Jonathan directly, David searched for a way to say "thank you" to his family for the kindness he'd received. He wanted to take the mentoring process full circle. He wanted to duplicate or multiply what he had been given.

There is little doubt in even a casual reading of scripture that David's closest friendship was with Jonathan. This peer-mentor had played an unforgettable role in David's life.

Jonathan had modeled what an available and trustworthy mentor should look like—and later, David felt he had no choice but to return the favor. He felt compelled to reproduce the investment in someone else. It couldn't just be anyone, however. David determined he would find a person fitted for the gift.

In II Samuel 9, we read how he made such a decision. Since Jonathan was now dead, David began to search for someone from *his household* that he could show kindness toward. He wanted to make deposits in the life of someone from the lineage of his mentor/ friend. Did anyone need help? Was anyone in trouble? Could anyone be in need of a mentor? Enter Mephibosheth.

When a servant directed King David to young Mephibosheth, the monarch called him in and offered him some incredible gifts and resources: the restoration of his grandfather's land to him; the invitation to dine at the King's table regularly; and unmerited esteem and kindness. The latter was even more significant because Mephibosheth was crippled. His physical handicap had all but ruined his self esteem (II Samuel 9:8). Mephibosheth had little regard for himself and had all but forgotten his royal heritage. But David hadn't.

In a nutshell, David did for Mephibosheth what Mephibosheth couldn't do for himself. This is a key lesson for mentors—giving to mentorees what they couldn't get by themselves, without help. Here are the tangible "resources" David gave to this particular mentoree:

1. David restored all that had belonged to King Saul to Mephibosheth

2. David mobilized servants to cultivate the land that he'd just given to Mephibosheth.

3. David provided food, income and a role as one of the King's sons.

This must have bolstered the confidence and self image of Mephibosheth. This kind of affirmation and undivided attention (especially to a lame man) from anybody would have been life changing—much less from someone of David's position of authority. Over time, Mephibosheth certainly must have began feeling like "somebody" again. What David was able to give was precisely what this mentoree needed to receive. Do you remember our working definition for "mentoring?" Mentoring is a relational experience where one person empowers another through the sharing of God-given resources. This is exactly what David did for this mentoree.

Mentoring Keys

THE MENTORING RELATIONSHIP: *King and Former Mentor's Son*

THE METHOD OF EMPOWERMENT: *Initiative; favor; esteem; a generous spirit*

THE GOD GIVEN RESOURCES: *Tangible gifts; restoration of confidence and self image; income; helpers (personnel).*

REFLECT AND RESPOND...

1. David broadens our "boundaries" for what we might typically call a "mentor." He gives to Mephibosheth so much more than mere words or wisdom. He gives him tangible gifts and resources (ie. people, revenue, land). What resources have you been given by influential people in your life?

2. How has your self esteem been raised by an influential person or mentor? What did they do? Have you been able to do this for someone else?

3. What resources do you have to offer, as a mentor? How might you give these to a mentoree?

4. What have you learned most from this episode between David and Mephibosheth?

NATHAN & DAVID

II Samuel 12

In his book, *Catch Me If You Can,* Frank Abagnale Jr. relays the tale of his wild and crazy life as a doctor, airline pilot, banker, investor, and celebrity. The irony behind his story is, that he wasn't any of these in reality. He deserves to receive an Academy Award for his portrayal of these professions. He was an intentional fake. A fraud. He was a pretender.

It all began quite early in his life when he realized he had the uncanny talent to convince people that he was "somebody" through his sheer confidence and acting ability. He began to make money at this "game" and soon found himself addicted to his pretending and role playing. Before it was all over, he'd performed a surgery in an operating room; conned banks out of thousands of dollars; flew an airplane as a pilot and gone places most of us only dream of going. The only problem was—it was all a show. It wasn't reality.

Unfortunately, many of us Christians become quite astute at the pretending game, as well. It's never as glamorous as the life of Frank Abagnale Jr., but we do it just the same. We pretend to be intimate with God; we pretend to be obedient in our evangelism and our tithing; we pretend to be "together" when we've chosen to live with a "pet sin" in our life. What's more, we're not alone. Throughout history, God's people have been "pretenders" who know what is right, but do the opposite—all the while never wanting to admit that they've done anything wrong. In II Samuel 12 we read about David's pretending game, and his need of a mentor who would force him to face the truth.

David is an interesting character. He seems to vacillate between mentoring others, and desperately needing a mentor, himself. He serves as a wonderful reminder to us that each of us ought to maintain a Paul (a mentor); a Barnabas (an accountability partner or peer mentor); and a Timothy (a mentoree) at all times in our lives.

His relationship with Nathan became absolutely essential, in the midst of his monarchy. David struggled a bit with his position as king, in II Samuel 11. During the season when "kings go out to battle"—David stayed at home, and remained idle. His inactivity led to a series of sins that included adultery, lying and deception, and murder. He needed some accountability from a trusted and respected mentor. God provided that mentor in Nathan.

The prophet Nathan fulfilled the most difficult role of a mentor: confrontation. Nathan is called upon by God to confront David, and the depth of his task is compounded by the fact that the sin has been committed by a visible leader. David's consequences, grief and embarrassment could not be kept private. It was not an enviable position for either of them. However, Nathan provides a marvelous model for mentors today, as he walks through the following principles in his interaction with David in II Samuel 12:

1. Affirmation (v.1) A personal visit by a priest/prophet demonstrated God's concern.
2. Objective frame of mind (v.1b-4) He spoke honestly having nothing to gain or lose.
3. Clear "truth telling" (v.7) He spoke forthrightly to David; he didn't mince words.
4. Reminders of his privileged position (v.7b-8) He solicited a right perspective.
5. Directly identifies the issue (v.9) He took the direct approach, risking no confusion.
6. Allows for response and feedback (v.5-6,13) He permitted David to respond to issues.
7. Establishes forgiveness (v.13b) He assures that he speaks God's forgiveness to David.
8. Communicates the consequences of his behavior (v.10-11,14) He doesn't waver.

9. Affirmation (v.24-25) He closes with words of encouragement and affirmation.

Two items should be noted about Nathan's confrontation of
David. First, he confronts boldly on this issue because it is blatant
and obvious. This is not a gray area, it is sin. It required direct
confrontation. (Clarification, rather than confrontation, should be
the mode of operation when the behavior in question is not a "sin".)
Second, Nathan initiated the contact. He didn't wait for his mentoree
to spot the problem. Initiative is a non-negotiable commodity for
good mentors. In this case, it paid tremendous dividends not only
for David, but for the entire nation of Israel. Tough mentoring
doesn't cost—it pays.

Mentoring Keys

THE MENTORING RELATIONSHIP: *Prophet and King
(both national, public leaders)*

THE METHOD OF EMPOWERMENT: *Direct dialogue and
instruction: "truth telling"*

THE GOD GIVEN RESOURCES: *Restored fellowship with
God; responsible behavior*

REFLECT AND RESPOND...

1. Nathan's chief contribution to David in II Samuel 12 is confrontation of sin. Why is confrontation so difficult? Why do we avoid
it so quickly?

2. List as many reasons as you can for why mentors must confront failures, sin, wrong attitudes, etc.? Review the above case study for insight.

3. Nathan had a clear gameplan when he confronted David. In the outline of this plan above, which step is easiest for you? Which is the most difficult?

4. When we must be confronted by a mentor, what can we learn from David's response to Nathan? Do you have any areas of your life that need confronting?

5. When the "issue" is not a sin, but a failure to meet an expectation or a goal—how might our approach to confrontation differ? (See the steps above.)

DAVID
& SOLOMON

I Kings 2:1-9, 3:6-14

I love the story of Jeremy who was taking a walk with his dad one night, after dark. Because he was only four years old, Jeremy held tightly to his father's hand. He knew the risk of falling into one of the many potholes in that road, and had been warned by his mother not to get dirty. After walking for just fifteen minutes, it happened. Jeremy stumbled and fell to the ground. Looking up from the pavement, Jeremy posed the question to his father: "Dad—why don't you watch where I'm going?"

This is a profound "life" question that I believe every son ought to ask their father, and every mentoree ought to ask their mentor. The fundamental role of the mentor is to watch where our protégés are heading in life. Then, that role expands to offering words of counsel and direction as they choose their paths. King David is a prime example.

In the midst of all of his failures, David accomplished a number of goals he'd set in his lifetime. One of those was to plan for the building of the temple, which he could not complete during his career. The second was to mentor his son Solomon and prepare him to finish the work he had begun. David could say with integrity that he was watching where Solomon was going.

One of the richest pictures in the Old Testament is seen when a father mentors his son. This took place on numerous occasions, but we see it vividly in the closing days of King David's reign, as he speaks to Solomon his son.

David embraced the principle: *success without a successor is a failure.* He wanted desperately for Solomon to be ready to follow in his steps as monarch. David "blessed" Solomon, as Hebrew fathers did; he spoke words to him that were both meaningful and memorable. Because of David's life, Solomon entered his career on a high. He could ride the "crest of the wave;" he shared his father's blessings and received the spoils of his father's conquests. I believe "blessing" our mentorees involves both *modeling* through the life we live, and *speaking* into their life, with our words.

On his deathbed, David issued a charge to his mentoree, and successor (I Kings 2). It was reminiscent of Moses' charge to Joshua before he died (Deuteronomy 31:23). In the first nine verses we see that his words were:

1. Words of Direction (v. 2-3)   3. Words of Trust (v. 5-7)
2. Words of Affirmation (v. 4)   4. Words of Remembrance (v. 8-9)

It is in the next chapter that we see a snapshot of the results of David's mentoring. In I Kings 3:6-14 Solomon responds to the "blessing" his mentor has given him. He both understands and acknowledges that his position of favor is due to his father's faithfulness to God. Indeed, he has observed and "caught" some tremendous qualities from his dad. David, for instance, had a "shepherd's heart;" a true heart for people that was *generous, compassionate* and *responsible.* This "heart" actually included a heart for all peoples and nations. Solomon embraced this same quality. In this chapter, he prays, and asks for a discerning spirit so that he might lead the people well (v. 6-9). This pleased the Lord, since Solomon asked for this above his own personal wealth, fame or long life (v. 10-14). Later in his career, the "nations" literally begin to visit him, as kings and queens from other lands observe his wisdom and power. He has caught and emulated the spirit of his mentor.

This *blessing* that was given to sons consisted of five elements. Gary Smalley and John Trent write about these elements in their book, *The Blessing.* The blessing includes:

1. *Spoken Words of Affirmation*
2. *Meaningful Touch*
3. *Expression of High Value*
4. *Word-Pictures of Their Future*
5. *Application of Genuine Commitment*

Solomon seems to have received most all of these from David. While he failed later in life, it likely was not due to the failure of his parents (mentors) to delight in him and show him favor. I am convinced that we, today, need to find ways to *bless* the mentorees that God has given us, either by nature (parents to children) or by choice (mentors to mentorees). Each of us need an authority figure in our lives who believes in us, and are committed to expressing that belief in tangible ways.

Mentoring Keys

THE MENTORING RELATIONSHIP: *Father and Son*

THE METHOD OF EMPOWERMENT: *Life model; proximity; favor; words of counsel*

THE GOD GIVEN RESOURCES: *Favor/loyalty; a successful heritage; a leadership position; and a heart for people*

REFLECT AND RESPOND...

1. David was concerned that Solomon as his successor carry on his faithfulness to God. What signs do you see in David's life and words for this passion? How can we express our spiritual "passion" to our mentorees?

2. What is the best way for us to prepare someone who will be our "successor" in a ministry or position of leadership? How is this different from Solomon's day?

3. Giving the "blessing" was part of the Jewish culture, in the Old Testament. Of the five elements listed above, which ones have you received from a parent/authority? Which ones have you failed to receive, even from a mentor?

4. How have you "blessed" others in your life? Have you given the elements of the blessing to a mentoree? What hinders you from doing so?

5. What is the most significant truth you learned from this mentoring relationship?

ELIJAH
& ELISHA
I Kings 19:19-21, II Kings 2:1-15

Some of the greatest mentors in history have also been some of the toughest. Often these mentors would test the staying power of their students by the assignments or advice they would give them. It was simply their way to evaluate how badly the mentorees really wanted to learn and grow.

One such mentor was Plato, who is among Greece's most famous philosophers. In the midst of a particularly grueling day with a class full of protégés, Plato looked up from his desk at the Academy to see how his students were processing the information he was dispensing. He had just finished reading and explaining one of his great dialogues, and knew it would be difficult for most of them to digest. He was not prepared, however, for what he saw.

There was only one student left in the class. The rest had fled, having surrendered all attempts to understand his wisdom. He could hardly believe that only one mentoree had what it took to stick it out. And who was this one remaining disciple? It was a young man named Aristotle. Perhaps that day Plato discerned that this one student was worth the investment of his life. Aristotle became at least as influential as his mentor, Plato.

Where did Plato learn this kind of "screening" process? According to Greek history, he likely learned it from his mentor, Socrates! The same kind of testing was used on him as a student— and once again, the "cream rose to the top." A man rises to the level he belongs.

And what happened to Aristotle? He went on to mentor a young, potential giant, named Alexander the Great! This ancient lineage of great leaders and philosophers (coincidentally) emerged not by accident, but through mentoring—just like what had happened in ancient Israel and Judah. Hundreds of years before Christ, a prophet named Elijah began a school to train Hebrew prophets. One, in particular, stood out. Like Plato and Aristotle, Elijah selected this young man to mentor, individually—and saw him rise above his peers.

One of the classic mentoring match-ups in the Old Testament is the one that occurred when Elijah met Elisha. Two fiery zealots, from two generations were matched up by God, Himself, to carry on a prophetic ministry designed to rid the land of Baal worship. You won't find a more *passionate* mentor than Elijah, anywhere. And, you'll be hard pressed to find a mentoree who *pursues* his mentor with any greater passion than Elisha.

In I Kings 19:19-21 we read how Elijah called Elisha to not only become a prophet, but to be his successor. Elijah was actually told to anoint three men to different offices, but the only one he got around to was the anointing of Elisha. It was his priority and focus to mentor this young emerging prophet, so that he could be the one to anoint the other men. Elisha immediately drops the plow he had in his hand, bids his family farewell, offers a sacrifice, and follows his new mentor. From his response, we see three marvelous protégé qualities:

1. He had *initiative*; he wasn't *idle* when he was called. He was busy.

2. He was *hungry*; he didn't *hesitate* when he was called. He had zeal.

3. He was *committed*; his goal wasn't *comfort* when called. He was surrendered.

This mentoree literally "runs after Elijah" his mentor! He is ready to sacrifice everything he is and has in order to be trained (in the office of a prophet), by this man who was known for being a Pioneer, a Trainer, a Defender, a Confronter, a Motivator and a Miracle Worker. Elijah throws his cloak around his mentoree as a sign of his vocation and authority. How empowering this must have been for this young man! Although Elijah had begun a "school of the prophets" which had trained at least 50-70 potential prophets, this man was to be the successor for the master. He left plowing fields to begin plowing "hearts."

Elijah must have taught Elisha everything he knew, for the two did not separate, even when Elijah was finally taken from his mentoree. When Elijah was told to go to Bethel, (one last time), he allowed Elisha to stay in the comfort of his home surroundings. He gave him this permission three times, but the mentoree would not leave his teacher. He was passionate and tenacious about receiving all he possibly could before his mentor departed. This last encounter the two would have, would ultimately prepare Elisha for the continuing work that awaited him. Finally, Elijah asked his mentoree what one, last request he had, before the two would be forced to part ways. Elisha boldly asked for a *double portion of his spirit.* II Kings 2:1-15 records this incredible episode. Elisha was asking for the "spiritual inheritance of the first-born son"(Deuteronomy 21:17). Elisha looked upon himself as the first born son, and even called Elijah "my father" as he mourned his departure (v.12). Although this was a request to continue the work of his mentor, Elijah knew that only God could grant that request— so he left it in God's hands.

God must have granted this bold and presumptuous request of Elisha, because his ministry emulated that of Elijah's, and then some. While Elijah's ministry was more *popular* because he was the prophet/pioneer, Elisha's may have been more *profound* as he performed approximately twice as many miracles as did his mentor.

Mentoring Keys

THE MENTORING RELATIONSHIP: *Prophet and Apprentice (student)*

THE METHOD OF EMPOWERMENT: *Instruction/admonishment; a ministry model to observe; time; approach able forum to ask questions*

THE GOD GIVEN RESOURCES: *His authority; esteem; tools for ministry; clear objectives*

REFLECT AND RESPOND...

1. Elijah and Elisha were almost "two peas in a pod." What are the advantages of finding a mentor or mentoree that is very similar to you? Are there disadvantages?

2. Most Bible commentators suggest that when Elijah gave Elisha his cloak (or mantle) he was calling him to be his successor as a prophet. What kinds of wonderful "esteem building" occur when we issue this authority to a mentoree? What dangers can occur?

3. Elisha was passionate about being mentored by Elijah. How can you demonstrate your spiritual passion and hunger to be trained, to your mentor?

4. When Elisha asked for a "double portion" of his mentor's spirit, Elijah couldn't grant that request, himself. He had to leave the answer in God's hands. How do we know when to back off and not give a straight answer to our mentoree? When is it right to not respond, and force them to simply trust God?

5. Elisha performed more miracles than his mentor. When your mentoree outperforms you—how do you respond? Why? How do you combat jealousy?

ELIJAH
& THE SCHOOL
OF THE PROPHETS

II Kings 2:3-18

In 1947, a professor at the University of Chicago, Dr. Chandrasekhar, was scheduled to teach an advanced seminar in astrophysics. At the time he was living in Wisconsin, doing research at the Yerkes astronomical observatory. He planned to commute twice a week for the class, even though it would be held during the harsh winter months.

Registration for the seminar, however, fell far below expectations. Only two students signed up the for the class. People expected Dr. Chandrasekhar to cancel, lest he waste his time. But for the sake of two students, he taught the class, commuting 100 miles round trip through back country roads in the dead of winter.

His students, Chen Ning Yang and Tsung-Dao Lee, did their homework. Ten years later, in 1957, they both won the Nobel prize for physics. So did Dr. Chandrasekhar in 1983. Perhaps the individual time and attention he was able to give made the difference in these two students. Certainly their professor became more of a mentor than just a teacher that semester. And for effective teacher/mentors—there is no such thing as a small class.

I believe the prophet Elijah embraced this truth, as he mentored some young apprentices during his ministry. He was committed to investing in his student-prophets. One reality we seldom remember from Old Testament days is that there were many more prophets than the ones we read about in the pages of scripture. These prophets were men who heard from God, served God, and made an impact in their day for God—but never wrote a book or were written about in a book included in the Bible.

These prophets were often discipled by a "master" who was more experienced in the office of a prophet, than they were. One such example was the "school of the prophets" which Elijah had established during his ministry. He was the *founder and chief mentor* of this training school. II Kings 2 records their existence, and relays at least two locations where they lived and studied: Bethel and Jericho. Elijah was the mentor/consultant and visited them regularly to speak into their lives, offer them correction and guidance, and get an update on how they were progressing. In fact, he was on his way to perform this very function, just before he was to be taken up by the chariots of fire, and depart the earth.

Elijah was a sort of "mentor-coach" to these men, for a number of reasons. One, he gave input but could not be with them in close proximity every day. He was a long-distance mentor, who had "up-close" contact for brief periods of time through his prophetic ministry. Two, there were several of these prophet-apprentices who were students in these schools. At least fifty followed him to the Jordan to watch his dramatic, fiery exit from earth. These same ones, interestingly, had been told by the Lord that he was going to leave *that very day.* Elijah must have taught them well, and must have selected and fostered men who had an evident gift— from the very beginning. They had even been informed in a pictorial fashion how it was going to happen (v.3). They were hearing from God and dictating what they heard in a prophetic manner. The formal structure that Elijah had established as a school was developing men *like him* to carry on the work of delivering the land from Baal worship—even after he was gone. Elijah was preparing to leave a legacy behind him.

On Elijah's last day on earth, these fifty men who followed both Elijah and Elisha, his chief apprentice, were called "sons of the prophets." They were intentional "observers" of their master, as often as they could be. They drew whatever truth/principles they could learn from their master—and his last day would be no different. They watched Elijah and Elisha from a distance as the two exchanged some last, intimate words in the final moments of Elijah's life. They were then *eye witnesses of the miraculous trans-*

lation of their master. He had fortified their lives once more, not only by his final visit to their home, but by allowing them to watch this concluding miracle in his own ministry. So concerned were they when it happened, that the fifty approached Elisha and asked permission to scour the land to see if the Spirit of God had taken up Elijah, only to cast him down somewhere in a nearby valley or mountain. They meticulously searched for him, but obviously didn't find him. It was, however, another clue as to their acute thirst to research and learn as much as they could, as long as they could! These mentorees had been coached by the best, and had proven to be *hungry* students, consuming all they could, in order to carry on the legacy Elijah had begun. Oh God, raise up such a school of mentorees today!

Mentoring Keys

THE MENTORING RELATIONSHIP: *Prophet and Student-Prophets (disciples)*

THE METHOD OF EMPOWERMENT: *Coaching; consulting; demonstration of ministry skills*

THE GOD GIVEN RESOURCES: *A model; prophetic ministry; personal convictions*

REFLECT AND RESPOND...

1. Elijah is a vivid example of a man who established a "mentoring structure" but oversaw his "school of the prophets" long distance. Do you have any *long distance mentors?* How have they impacted your life?

2. How must a mentoree change his/her approach to a mentor, if they are only present for brief periods of time? When the mentoring is long distance, should the mentoree initiate more often? Should they come up with questions to ask during the meeting time? How might it look? What are the advantages and disadvantages of this?

3. How did these men from the "school of the prophets" prove to be *model* mentorees?

4. Elijah had quite a task to fulfill in training so many who were a part of the "school of the prophets." How would you handle the mentoring of 50-75 people who wanted to be trained and mentored by you?

5. What is the chief lesson or insight you've gained from this mentoring relationship?

JEHOIADA  & JOASH

II Kings 12, II Chronicles 24

At the turn of the twentieth century, there was a family living in Europe that began to experience many of the same problems that our families face today. There were fights taking place between mom and dad; the kids were slipping with their grades at school and straying in their activities after school. The scenario became what we would call "dysfunctional" today. The Schicklewuber family certainly had their share of conflict.

One evening, the husband and wife began to argue in the kitchen. Listening to their conversation from the next room was their young son. Suddenly and with great passion, Mr. Schicklewuber declared that they should move and get away from this mess they were in. His wife agreed. What their son perceived, however, was that the two parents were planning to abandon him, and leave town. He was devastated.

Immediately, he put his emotional guard up and determined that no one could hurt him anymore with their threats...not even mom or dad. He was going to make it alone. Soon, his heart began to grow bitter and resentful, and in his teen years he was a troubled young man—but he wouldn't let anyone in to help.

It is a shame, because that young man grew up to spew his own emotional poison and perspective on millions of people across Europe during the next two decades. You know this man as Adolf Hitler.

I have wondered what might have happened had this young boy had a dad (or any other mentor for that matter) really demonstrate care and concern for him; to help him fight his battles as a son so he wouldn't feel he had to fight so many as an adult. Unfortunately, sometimes even when there is a mentor—people don't always grow from them. Maybe Adolf Hitler's father actually *did* try to invest in his son, but was a "day late and a dollar short." Sometimes good mentors don't produce well because they just don't have a responsive mentoree.

Such was the case with Jehoiada and Joash. Although their story may be less familiar than others in the Old Testament, there is much to be learned from the mentoring that Jehoiada provided for King Joash. Jehoiada served as high priest during the first several years of Joash's monarchy. He was a needed mentor, since Joash became king at the age of seven.

However, volumes of information is communicated and implied about the mentoring of Joash. Jehoiada possessed the qualities of a good mentor which spell the word GOAL:

> **G- Godliness** (He was spiritually sound; did what was right)
> **O- Objectivity** (He could see the right and the wrong clearly)
> **A- Authenticity** (He was genuine and real, wherever he was)
> **L- Loyalty** (He was committed to those in his care)

Unfortunately, Joash never gleaned those qualities, as his mentoree. II Chronicles 24:14 tells us that he (and the people) offered burnt offerings *so long as Jehoiada lived.* When Jehoiada died, so did the spirit of reformation. King Joash seemingly was as quick to do evil *after his mentor's death,* as he was to do good before. He is a vivid example of a mentoree who performs well when *he is supervised,* but not on his own. While being mentored, King Joash oversaw the restoration of the temple, the offerings given by the people and the cessation of idol worship. That was as far as he could go with his mentor. Without a mentor, Joash allowed idol worship, killed Jehoiada's son, was overtaken by an invading army, and was assassinated in the campaign. Oh, how quickly we forget our lessons.

Joash failed as a mentoree in the following ways. Although he was influenced by his mentor—even to the point that he acted on the counsel he received, he was only *influenced* but not *impacted.* By this I mean he did right as long as his mentor was present, but failed to pass it on, once Johoiada was gone (II Kings 12:2). He forgot the kindness of his mentor, and all that he owed to God on account of him. Jehoiada had saved the life and throne of Joash, preserved the royal house of David for the monarchy and had helped put an end to Judah's idolatry. When confronted by his mentor's own son years later (for his disobedience), he was so far gone that he had him stoned to death!

Jehoiada failed as a mentor in the following ways. Although he tried, he was not able to give "ownership" of truth to his mentoree. Perhaps this was because of the hard heart or the weak character of Joash, but Jehoiada could not move his mentoree from raw obedience to ownership. He gave him the *rules* but did not *reproduce* himself in Joash. Nothing seemed to be transferable. We must remember: the objective of the mentor must always be to work himself out of a job! Minimally, this means two things must happen:

1. *They must give ownership of truth (The mentor is not needed as a supervisor)*
2. *The mentoree can and will reproduce it in others (When the mentor is departed)*

When mentors cannot accomplish this, then they do not leave a legacy behind! All we have is what is achieved as long as we are around. We've only influenced one generation. May God grant to us "multiplying mentorees" for generations to come.

Mentoring Keys

THE MENTORING RELATIONSHIP: *High Priest and King*

THE METHOD OF EMPOWERMENT: *Spiritual counsel and direction; support; protection; cooperative effort and shared goals; vocationally*

THE GOD GIVEN RESOURCES: *Spiritual covering; wisdom; boundaries; and his team of priests to carry out the revenue collection for the temple*

REFLECT AND RESPOND...

1. Joash, the *mentoree*, was King of Judah. When our mentoree has a high profile position, how should we approach the task of a mentor? Are we to do anything differently?

2. As stated above, Joash never internalized the "truth" he got from Jehoiada. He only practiced it when his mentor was present. How do we know when our mentoree really "owns" what we are passing to them? How can we insure that they do?

3. As a mentoree, what can we do to safeguard against the *trap* that Joash fell into: the trap of "people pleasing" instead of "God pleasing?" How do we "own" truth for ourselves?

4. In the account above, the mentor and mentoree shared a common goal: the repair of the temple. They had a common task to accomplish. What are the advantages of sharing a task in a mentoring relationship? What are the disadvantages?

5. What can we do to accomplish genuine "spiritual reproduction" in others?

ISAIAH
& HEZEKIAH

Isaiah 37:21-35, 38:4-8, II Chronicles 32:20

When Nancy was well into her forties, she happened to attend a high school reunion in her home town. There, she met her former music teacher whom she hadn't seen for many years. Nancy knew she had to express her gratitude for the many hours the instructor had invested in her, so without a further thought she began to elaborate on how much it had meant to her to have such a mentor, musically. Nancy thanked her for her patience, her gifts, her ability to pass on a concept and a skill to teens—and how her own love for music had flourished because of this experience.

Her teacher did not know what to say. This acknowledgement and recognition was new for her. After turning a few shades of red, the instructor simply said, "Nancy, thank you for the words of gratitude and encouragement. You have made my day!"

To that, Nancy appropriately responded, "No—thank you! You have made my life!"

This kind of gratitude is far too rare. Seldom do we take the opportunity to thank the mentors God has sent us through our lives. These very words, however, that Nancy articulated to her teacher— "You have made my life!"—could have easily been spoken by King Hezekiah to his spiritual mentor Isaiah following their shared experience.

The developmental relationship that evolved between Isaiah, the prophet, and King Hezekiah was a beautiful and almost classic example of the power of God-given authority. Hezekiah, who happened to be the king of Judah, earnestly sought after Isaiah requesting that he speak into his life as a spiritual mentor, during days of crises in his monarchy.

Early in Isaiah 37, Hezekiah hears that the king of Assyria has executed an attack on all the fortified cities in the land of Judah.

The name of Yahweh has been blasphemed, and Hezekiah responds by tearing his robes and covering himself with sackcloth. Immediately, he sends some servants to seek out Isaiah. Hezekiah, who may have been an adequate king during his day—knew that he needed some spiritual counsel from a mentor who was in touch with God. This was no longer merely a political or sociological issue. He needed some expertise from a prophet. (Often, this kind of scenario can be a clear signal for us, as well, to seek out a mentor who has specific expertise in an area outside our strengths.)

According to II Chronicles 32:20, Isaiah and Hezekiah connected and passionately sought the Lord together. Isaiah modeled absolute dependency on God for his authority, and wasn't ashamed to do so in the presence of his political leader. He identifies with the distress of his king, but finds it within himself to *"change hats"* and become his personal mentor. We see Isaiah *speaking into the life* of his mentoree on two vivid occasions. First, in Isaiah 37:21-35 where he addresses the military and spiritual attack on Judah and her God; then again in Isaiah 38:1-8 where he warns Hezekiah that he must get his house in order, for his imminent death. In these two case studies, we observe three principles from the mentoring style of Isaiah. They are the clearest demonstrations of *spiritual authority* that we see in all of the Old Testament, between a mentor and a mentoree:

1. *Isaiah speaks with divine authority.* This mentor is not afraid to say "thus saith the Lord" to his mentoree. And because he speaks with such divine foundations, he can be objective and forthright in his counsel. When he doesn't know what to say next, he seeks the Lord; when he does have a word from the Lord—he speaks with deep spiritual power. This enabled Isaiah to mentor others with deep conviction.

2. *Isaiah speaks with definite assertiveness.* This second principle is a result of the first. Isaiah received a word from the Lord for Hezekiah, and asserted himself boldly in his conversation with his mentoree. In chapter 37 it was a word of affirmation. That's

good news. In chapter 38 it was a word of admonition. That's not so good news. In either case, however, Isaiah wasn't sheepish or withdrawn. There was no cowardice in him. This enabled Isaiah to mentor with great boldness.

3. *Isaiah speaks with direct aim and ambition.* Fortunately, Isaiah didn't speak with such aggressiveness just to appear powerful, or to project a prophetic image. He had a clear objective in mind: he wanted to elicit proper attitudes and obedience from his mentoree. It appears that he was successful, too. After informing his mentoree that he was to die soon, Hezekiah is moved to brokenness and repentance. God sees/hears his cry, and determines to allow him to live for another fifteen years. Isaiah's words drew the right *heart response* from his mentoree, because he used them as "goads" (Ecclesiastes 12:11). This enabled him to mentor with clear direction.

Mentoring Keys

THE MENTORING RELATIONSHIP: *Prophet and King*

THE METHOD OF EMPOWERMENT: *Words of truth, spoken in love; prophetic authority; modeled dependency on God; integrity*

THE GOD GIVEN RESOURCES: *Divine assurance and guidance; spiritual convictions; physical healing and restoration*

REFLECT AND RESPOND...

1. The most obvious trademark of Isaiah's mentoring style was deep authority, when he spoke. How does a mentor gain that kind of authority? Does it come from God, or is it something that a mentoree decides they ought to give to you, as the mentor?

2. What indicators does the scripture give us that Hezekiah was a man who sought after the truth? (Hint: look at his choice for a mentor!) How can we fall in love with truth, today, more than self promotion or preservation?

3. Would having a mentor like Isaiah, who hears God's voice so clearly, scare you or attract you, as a mentoree? Why?

4. As mentors, why do we struggle so much with speaking into the lives of our mentorees? Why do we wrestle with having spiritual authority?

5. What is the greatest lesson you've learned from Isaiah and Hezekiah's relationship?

LUKE
& THEOPHILUS
Luke 1:1-4, Acts 1:1-3

In Judaism, there is an old tradition that took place whenever a young boy first began to read and study. The very day that he reads his first word from the Torah, he is given a taste of honey. This is so he will always associate *learning* with *sweetness.* From that point on that Hebrew boy connects the experience of personal study and growth with the wonderful taste of honey. Learning does not have to be labor, they believed. It is our friend.

It should be the same with us. We should hunger to learn like we hunger for dessert. We should associate the acquisition of knowledge with pleasure and benefit. This is the kind of ideology Luke, the Gospel writer, must have embraced as he wrote to Theophilus and mentored him with his literary narratives.

We know very little about the mentoring relationship between Luke and Theophilus. All we do know for sure is that Luke felt a very acute and personal responsibility to teach his mentoree all the basics of the life of Jesus and His early Church.

Scholars may disagree as to how much "face to face" contact Luke had with Theophilus, but because both the Gospel of Luke and the Book of Acts are addressed directly to this man, Luke must have done much of his mentoring *through the mail!* He is a wonderful example of a "long distance mentor." His use of the pen and the written word was most profound and influential not only on Theophilus but on the rest of us, as well! He is an illustration of the fact that we can mentor both from a distance and from a different time period! Luke left a legacy because he left his informative words on paper. The following list are truths concerning the mentoring style and impact of Dr. Luke:

HE WAS INTIMATE. In the opening paragraph of both *Luke* and *Acts*, he refers directly to Theophilus. It appears his goal wasn't to write a best-seller for his generation, but to personally address the spiritual needs of his mentoree. His personal salutation enables the information to become more relevant to his intended reader, even when in written form.

HE WAS INTENTIONAL. In Luke 1:4 he states his purpose: that Theophilus might know the exact truth about Jesus. He is the only writer to record the Gospel "in consecutive order" (Luke 1:3). He was deliberate and purposeful about everything he put into his "story;" it wasn't just a scrap of words to prove he knew his subject well.

HE WAS INVESTIGATIVE. Luke mentions that he had "investigated everything." One translation said he "followed all things closely" or he "tracked down" the information. He admits he was *not* an eyewitness, but commentators agree he was in a favored position to obtain it from people like John Mark, Philip, the prophet Agabus and Silas.

HE WAS INTUITIVE. This quality made him an exceptional mentor. Luke was a physician which must have given him an edge on anticipating the needs of those to whom he ministered. He laid out the narratives in both of his books in order to address the issues he sensed his mentoree must have had questions about, or simply needed to hear.

HE WAS INSTRUCTIONAL. No doubt Luke wanted to inform and instruct his mentoree since he admits that "many have undertaken to compile an account of the things that were accomplished among us" (Luke 1:1). He surely had further items he wanted to elaborate on, and teach Theophilus, that Mark's short account didn't cover. He wanted to educate.

HE WAS INDELIBLE. This is one of the hallmarks of Luke's mentoring style. Unlike so many others in his culture, Luke used the "written word." He chose his words carefully and wisely. This made his mentoring memorable, since his mentoree could return to the words over and over again. With his words in print, Luke forever left a legacy behind him.

HE WAS ILLUSTRATIVE. Luke is considered one of the most accurate historians of his day. His writing contained vivid descriptions and detail. He knew how to tell a story, and paint a picture in the mind of his mentoree. Indeed, he painted the "big picture," through his books, of the Savior of the whole earth, in a way that no one could miss.

HE WAS INSPIRING. This mentor enabled his reader to *experience* Jesus, through his narratives. His speech was moving. He captured the humanity and compassion of Jesus in such a way that his mentoree must have felt empowered. The name *Theophilus* means "lover of God." Mentor Luke enabled this mentoree to incarnate that God-given name.

Mentoring Keys

THE MENTORING RELATIONSHIP: *Physician/Missionary and Friend*

THE METHOD OF EMPOWERMENT: *The written word; personal concern; a teacher's heart*

THE GOD GIVEN RESOURCES: *Two detailed teaching narratives, personally investigated and written to his mentoree*

REFLECT AND RESPOND...

1. Luke did much of his mentoring through the printed page. List

the ways this proves that one can mentor another from a distance.

2. Luke left a legacy for Theophilus, long after he had died. What are the advantages of putting "truth" in print? What are the disadvantages of having them in print *alone?*

3. From the list of Luke's mentoring style, above, which do you feel would have the greatest impact on a mentoree? Which ones do you do well?

4. What are the benefits of being a great *story teller*, for a mentor? Have any of your past mentors painted pictures in your mind that have lingered over the years? Which ones?

5. What stands out as the greatest lesson for you, from this mentoring relationship?

ELIZABETH & MARY

Luke 1:36-56

A college professor had his sociology class go into the Baltimore slums to gather case histories of 200 young boys. They were asked to write an evaluation of each boy's future. In every case the students wrote: "He hasn't got a chance." Twenty five years later another sociology professor came across the earlier study. He had his students follow up on the project to see what had happened to these boys.

With the exception of twenty boys who had moved away or died, the students learned that 176 of the remaining 180 had achieved extraordinary success as lawyers, doctors and businessmen.

The professor was astounded and decided to pursue the matter further. Fortunately, all the men were in the area and he was able to ask each one, "How do you account for your success?" In each case the reply came with feeling: "There was a teacher..."

The teacher was still alive, so he sought her out and asked the old but still alert lady what magic formula she had used to pull these boys out of the slums into successful achievement.

The teacher's eyes sparkled and her lips broke into a gentle smile. "It's really very simple," she said. "I loved those boys."

Indeed, love is the most powerful force in the world. Each of us need it more than material possessions or many of the daily luxuries at our fingertips. It transforms and empowers when force cannot. Perhaps this is the reason why Mary sought out her cousin Elizabeth when she discovered she was going to give birth to the Messiah. Elizabeth simply had love and understanding to offer to her, as her mentor.

This story begins with Mary receiving an astonishing visit by the angel, Gabriel. It was a divine encounter that changed her life:

she was going to give birth to the Messiah. It must have been a dream come true for her; it was the hope of every Jewish girl in those days.

In Luke 1:39-45 we see how Luke puts this divine encounter in the context of a very human encounter. What did Mary do after this earth-shaking experience with Gabriel? She immediately ran off to tell Elizabeth, her cousin. She couldn't wait to share what had happened with a significant person in her life. You can just imagine Elizabeth's response: "Tell me about it! What happened? Then what did Gabriel say? And what did you say?" How much we all need mentors like Elizabeth to share the *watershed moments* of our lives. Both Elizabeth (the mentor) and Mary (the mentoree) are beautiful illustrations of the principle of *availability.* They were available to each other in the key seasons of their lives. In fact, I believe there are at least four reasons why Elizabeth was a *good mentor* for Mary, and as many reasons why Mary was a *good mentoree* for Elizabeth.

WHY ELIZABETH WAS A GOOD MENTOR FOR MARY...

1. She was a step ahead of Mary in her own journey. Elizabeth also had a miraculous baby in her own womb, and was six months pregnant. She was only a few paces ahead of Mary, and teaches us that *we* don't need to be miles ahead of our mentorees.

2. She shared common experiences with Mary. Not only were both facing the birth of an unexpected son, but both had been visited by Gabriel. Perhaps Elizabeth had shared this visitation with Mary earlier, and now Mary could benefit from her story and experience.

3. She understood Mary and fostered her obedience. Elizabeth was not jealous, even though she admitted that Mary's baby would be greater than her own. She spoke a word of blessing to Mary and affirmed everything she was going through.

4. She modeled Spirit-filled living in the face of unfamiliar

territory. Mary could draw upon Elizabeth's experience. Luke 1:41-42 tells us that Elizabeth "was filled with the Holy Spirit...and she spoke..." Neither one of these women had been through this experience before; Mary must have watched her mentor closely for cues as to her own life response.

Why Mary Was A Good Mentoree For Elizabeth...

1. She took initiative and pursued Elizabeth. Good mentorees always display their hunger and passion for personal growth. Mary traveled for miles from Galilee to the hill country, and stayed with Elizabeth to gain whatever she could from her mentor.

2. She was humble and teachable. Mary greeted Elizabeth, then the remaining text relays how her mentor spoke into her life, confirming that what had been prophesied would, indeed, come to pass. Although Mary would bear the Messiah, she played the role of a teachable mentoree when it came to her older cousin. She listened before she spoke.

3. She wanted God's will for her life more than anything. Mary demonstrated through her discourse (known as the "magnificat" in vs. 46-55) that she simply wanted *God's agenda* not *her agenda.* This attitude provides moist and fertile "soil" for the mentor to garden.

4. She gave her mentor time. After their initial meeting, Luke 1:56 records that Mary stayed with Elizabeth for three solid months, through the birth of John! I like to speculate what they talked about during those three months. I'm sure they covered everything—God, angels, babies, Israel and the world. They shared life.

What a model these two women were for becoming available to one another. In this time, they prepared their hearts for participation in events that would literally change the world.

Mentoring Keys

THE MENTORING RELATIONSHIP: *Cousins (elder and younger)*

THE METHOD OF EMPOWERMENT: *Time; sharing her own experience; affirmation; a life model*

THE GOD GIVEN RESOURCES: *Availability; a refuge (a classroom for learning); wisdom*

REFLECT AND RESPOND...

1. Elizabeth and Mary seemed to be "two peas in a pod." How can so many common experiences work for mutual advantage in a mentoring relationship? How can they become a negative factor?

2. Do you have someone that shares your dreams and lifestyle so similarly? How has God used them to change your life?

3. Elizabeth wasn't jealous even though she knew Mary's son would become far "greater" than her own. How does a mentor maintain perspective in these kinds of situations?

4. In the devotional thoughts above, we discovered that Elizabeth was merely a few paces ahead of Mary, in her own journey. How does this liberate you to mentor others more frequently? What advantages are gained from being so close in the pace of the journey?

John The Baptizer
& His Disciples

John 1:29-42, 3:22-30

Mₒᵣₑ than thirty years ago, actor Fred MacMurray starred in a delightful movie, entitled: "Follow Me Boys." Although it was filmed in black and white, the story carried some timeless and universal truths.

As the plot unfolds, we meet a gentleman who reluctantly is called upon to lead a young scouting group. These boys have no intention of following him, however, and instead become sources of chaos and confusion for him. Add to this the competition this scout leader experiences with other adults and interests in their lives—and it becomes plain that this wanna-be leader will never achieve the boys' loyalty or allegiance.

Yet, as the story draws to a close, he does win their affection and commitment. By the end of the movie, the scout leader is hiking on a trail with his loyal protégés following right behind him, like apprentices emulating a master. The scout leader has won their hearts through demonstrating his own sheer commitment and character. His love and passion for the boys and the "cause" proved to them he was a man worth following.

If John the Baptizer were to make a Hollywood film, he could have used the same title: "Follow Me Boys." He also could have used the same basic plot. He was a mentor who won the hearts of his disciples by the way he lived his life.

One of the most intriguing but misunderstood mentors of the New Testament was John the baptizer. Jesus described him as "more than a prophet" and later said he was the greatest man born of a woman. That's quite a compliment!

Interestingly, John was one of many who was actually making disciples, before Jesus ever showed up on the scene. He had been mentoring a group of young men for some time, when he spotted Jesus one day, in the early part of his own disciple-making ministry. It was at this point that we observe the most remarkable truth from John's mentorship: He was secure enough to release his own mentorees to a Mentor who was better suited to take them to their next step. In this case, that next mentor was Jesus, Himself (John 1:29-42).

As a mentor, he must have been extraordinary. His ministry emphasis was *authenticity* and *commitment*. He focused on calling people to *demonstrate with their life* that they were taking God seriously, not just with their words or synagogue attendance. He was prophetic in his style and saw things as very "black and white." Doubtless, this colored the way he must have demanded integrity, convictions and excellence from his mentorees. He had them observe and even participate in baptizing people for repentance. He must have been a stickler as a mentor; an impassioned driver of his students.

At the same time, he had a very tender and humble side. He understood truth objectively and gave godly perspective to his mentorees. For instance, when they came to him complaining that "other disciples" were also baptizing converts, John reminded them that no authority was given to anyone except by God, and that *He(God)* was the source of true mentoring (John 3:25-30). In addition, we see his human side when he is thrown in prison years later. By this time, he has given away most all of his mentorees to Jesus, and he experiences some of his own doubts about the Kingdom. He voices these doubts to Jesus, through some of his remaining, loyal protégés (Matthew 11:2-3). It is at this point that Jesus affirms John's unique role as a leader and mentor.

Three observations stand out regarding John's leadership/mentoring ministry for us today:

1. He understood his own calling and task: to call the people of Israel to repent, and to prepare the way for Jesus' ministry. He was clear on his own identity.

2. He understood who he was *not*: several times he verified that he was not the Messiah or the Lamb of God. (Incidentally, it's amazing simply to have been mistaken for Jesus!) He said, "He must increase but I must decrease." He was secure concerning his ego.

3. He understood his contribution to the "big picture;" he was to simply *point* the way, not *be* the way. He literally gave up his mentorees when he had done all he could with them, and turned them over to become Jesus' mentorees. He was honest about his role.

Andrew was a brilliant example of this last observation. In John 1:29-42 we read about John pointing out who Jesus was to his mentorees. Andrew is obviously encouraged to make the "switch" to Jesus, and quickly begins asking Him questions. He later finds his brother Peter, and leads him to Christ. All of this could've been a real source of envy and frustration to John—but it wasn't. This mentor simply gave what he had, never assuming he should do any more or less. He is a model of security and identity for us all.

Mentoring Keys

THE MENTORING RELATIONSHIP: *Prophet and Disciples (students)*

THE METHOD OF EMPOWERMENT: *Demonstration of convictional ministry; instruction; direction; participation in baptisms; humble identity*

THE GOD GIVEN RESOURCES: *"Big picture" perspective; ministry experience; objectivity on truth*

REFLECT AND RESPOND...

1. When John saw Jesus in the presence of his mentorees, he affirmed His ministry and encouraged his mentorees to follow Jesus. What allowed John to be able to do this? How well do you allow your mentorees to be free to find other mentors?

2. How do you know when it is time to terminate a mentoring relationship? Are there tangible signals to look for?

3. Jot down exactly why mentors must settle the issue of their own *identity* and *personal security,* before they intentionally influence a mentoree.

4. As a mentoree, do you have a clear idea of what you *need* from a mentor? Do you know who can provide it for you? As a mentor, do you know what you have to offer a mentoree? Write down your response to both of these, below.

5. By observing the manner which John the baptizer related to his mentorees, we can see that he had *their* best interests in mind, not his own. How can we demonstrate this to our mentorees (or mentors) today?

BARNABAS
& SAUL

Acts 9:26-30

Sir Humphry Davy was a distinguished chemist of the nineteenth century. When he was asked late in his life what he considered to be his greatest discovery—he replied: "Michael Faraday." And, indeed, he had been the one who found young Faraday.

Davy had discovered Michael Faraday, the ignorant son of a blacksmith, taking notes at his lectures and longing to study science seriously. As Davy began to teach him, he found a brilliant mind that promised to eclipse even his own achievements. He knew that no one discovery of his own could possibly compare with the many discoveries Faraday would make during his career. Hence, his investment became a personal one into a "life," not a laboratory.

This "discovery" must have been rewarding to Davy. It is illustrative of the feeling that Barnabas must have had when he first met Saul, who later became Paul the Apostle. It must have been clear to him that Saul had the potential to become one of the greatest leaders of the Church—perhaps even eclipsing his own influence. Consequently, Barnabas saw his investment in him as strategic ministry.

Too few Christians realize that before Paul and Barnabas became traveling companions on their first missionary journey—Barnabas was actually a mentor for young Paul (still known as Saul in his early days). Barnabas became famous for taking on the needs of certain disciples and ministering to them, giving them whatever resources they needed until they could get on their feet (Acts 4:34-37). Such was the case with he and Saul.

Three years after his conversion, Saul was still between a rock and a hard place. Although Ananias had built a "bridge" for Saul in Damascus (between him and the local church), the folks in Jerusalem were not so quick to receive him. The Jews considered him a traitor and an apostate (they later even tried to kill him for this); while the believers in Jerusalem couldn't trust him. He had been their public enemy number one (Acts 9:26). Saul needed another "bridge builder." Enter his mentor, Barnabas.

Barnabas, which means "Son of Encouragement," once again lived up to his name. He put his own relationship with the Apostles on the line by embracing Saul. In Acts 9:27 we read: "But Barnabas took hold of him and brought him to the Apostles..." The Greek words actually imply that *he took Saul by the hand* and led him in before the Apostles to affirm his belief in him, his conversion and his new life in Christ. How did Barnabas know all this? How could he be sure? I believe it is because he sought Saul out when he first arrived in the city. He had to know firsthand. And when he did, he became the reconciler, the enabler, the intercessor...the "bridge builder." Barnabas is the classic illustration of a mentor who *truly believed in his mentoree.* He was the initiator in the relationship. In doing so, I believe he shows us what happens when a mentor believes deeply in someone:

He represented Saul before significant contacts. One of the gifts Barnabas gave his mentoree was to introduce him and even represent him before some very key people: the Apostles. According to Acts 9:27 he spoke on behalf of Saul. He was a sort of spiritual agent! He gave him credibility when Saul had not been around long enough to earn it himself. He put him in touch with the leaders who could make or break him in that city.

He defended Saul against significant criticism. A second gift Barnabas gave to Saul was to defend him, when he likely wouldn't have been heard by his accusers. Again, in verse 27 he "described how he (Saul) had seen the Lord...and how He had talked to him, and how at Damascus he had spoken out boldly in the name of Jesus." Barnabas believed his report and patiently quieted his critics in Jerusalem. What a gift.

He supported Saul amidst significant challenges. A third gift Barnabas gave was amazing favor and support. He became

Saul's biggest fan in Jerusalem! He championed his call and ministry. He was a "grace giver" when Saul needed grace the most. In Acts 9:28-30 we read that Saul eventually moved with the Apostles speaking out boldly and ministering alongside of them. He had been accepted! During his stay, however, the Jews plotted an attempt on his life. When Barnabas and the others learned about it, they *all* helped him depart safely from Jerusalem to Tarsus. We all need someone to believe in us like this; if only we all had a Barnabas!

One of the necessary requirements of such a mentor role is great *personal security*. Barnabas was secure in his identity and his position in the church. He understood his role. Consequently, when Saul later became Paul—the famous church planter and authority of the Gentile church, Barnabas was still able to affirm and support him as a *colleague*, even when he (Saul) didn't "need" him anymore. I believe we cannot enable others (externally) until we embrace this kind of security (internally). We can't be a *grace giver* until we are a *grace receiver!*

Mentoring Keys

THE MENTORING RELATIONSHIP: *Church Leader and Emerging Leader (new Christian)*

THE METHOD OF EMPOWERMENT: *Belief in the person; initiative; understanding/mercy; encouragement; wise counsel*

THE GOD GIVEN RESOURCES: *Wisdom; personal support; divine contacts with key people; a sense of belonging*

REFLECT AND RESPOND...

1. Barnabas believed in Saul before the other Jerusalem leaders did. What enables a mentor to believe so deeply in a mentoree?

2. Barnabas had a track record of helping/empowering the "under-dog." Who do you know that fits this description that you could support? How could you help them?

3. One of the greatest gifts Barnabas gave to Saul was some divine contacts with key leaders in the Church. Why was this so significant? How have mentors in your past done this with you? Who could you introduce to an up and coming mentoree?

4. As soon as Barnabas heard him debate the Jewish leaders, he must have known that Saul was destined for fame in influence in his ministry. Jot down what inner qualities you believe enabled Barnabas to still support him instead of envy him?

BARNABAS
& JOHN MARK

Acts 12:25, 15:37-39, II Timothy 4:11

Kent Amos, the former Xerox executive and more recently head of the Washington based Urban Family Institute, once said, "We never think of helping troubled young people to change their lives, by giving them the guidance and education and training they need. Instead, we think punitively: three strikes and your out; two years and you're off welfare—even if you have no place else to go."

Tony Campolo tells the story of an elementary school teacher, named Miss Thompson. One year she had a student in her class named Teddy Stollard. Teddy was a troubled young boy, who often was a source of disruption and in need of discipline. Miss Thompson was at the end of her rope in December, when Teddy brought her a crudely wrapped gift. She opened it and found a necklace (with some of the pearls missing) and a half empty bottle of perfume. When his classmates began to laugh, Miss Thompson quickly told him she really appreciated both of the gifts. After class, Teddy lingered. "I'm glad you liked the necklace, Miss Thompson," he muttered. "And—you smell just like my mother did."

After Teddy left, Miss Thomspon quickly checked the records of his last four years. Suddenly, it all made sense. She discovered that in first grade, Teddy's mother became ill; by the second grade she had died; and the year prior his home life became increasingly unstable, his father being unable to work and raise the kids by himself. In short, life was a mess for young Teddy. Immediately, Miss Thompson recognized her role as a mentor to him, not just a school teacher. The rest of the year—she was amazed at how well he responded to her increased attention.

To make a long story short, she had changed this young boy's life. He never forgot her. When he graduated from high school, he wrote to her, thanking her for helping him to believe in himself. When he graduated from college, he wrote saying, "I'll bet you never thought I'd make it this far!" Again, he expressed his gratitude. Four years later, he wrote again:

"Dear Miss Thompson—believe it or not, I graduate from medical school in one month. I am graduating at the top of my class. Thank you for all that you've meant to me over years. You have made up for what I seemed to lack at home. In fact...I have a favor to ask. I am getting married this summer. Would you honor me with your presence— and would you sit in the seat where my mother would have sat, if she were still alive?"

Miss Thompson wiped the tears from her eyes. She ended up attending, and filling the role Teddy had requested of her. She deserved to do so. She'd become an invaluable mentor to him; she'd believed in him when no one else did—and had changed his life.

This was the story of Barnabas and John Mark. Barnabas became a mentor for this young man who desperately needed someone to believe in him. Their story is nothing short of incredible.

Sometime after they returned from their first missionary journey, Paul challenged Barnabas to join him on a second trip to follow up on their new churches and converts. They agreed that this second effort would be beneficial to everyone involved—but that's as far as the harmony went. The two of them encountered conflict and disagreement regarding the one item big enough to prevent them from any further mutual missionary work. Of all things, this disagreement was over an emerging mentoring relationship that was developing between Barnabas and John Mark.

During their first mission trip, John Mark had joined the team (Acts 12:25). He was young and inexperienced, but I'm sure relished the opportunity for adventure and to write some more of the accounts of these early church leaders. When they arrived in Pamphylia, however, he deserted them. Apparently, the ministry was too tough for John Mark.

This is where the disagreement arose. Barnabas had gotten to know Mark, firsthand, just like he had done with Saul. He grew to love and believe in him. He wanted to take Mark with them on the second journey to "give him a second chance." Paul saw no wisdom in this. He was dead weight. He would need to *be ministered to* rather than be able to *minister.* It was black and white to Paul. So, they parted ways (Acts 15:36-40).

The lesson we learn from Barnabas' conviction to separate from Paul so that he could mentor John Mark is this: *Few ever reach their potential unless someone else wants them to.* No one peaks in their performance until another really believes in them. To be honest, this is a consistent truth taught by Barnabas and every mentoree with whom he relates. He was a man who *brought out the best in people* because he believed in them; he saw raw potential in them even when no one else did.

What enabled Barnabas to practice this kind of people-optimism? From the passages we read about him, the following points and patterns surface over and over again:

1. LOOK FOR INNER-POTENTIAL NOT THEIR IMPERFECTIONS
Anyone can spot flaws and walk away; mentorees need mentors who see the invisible.

2. AFFIRM ANY STEP FORWARD; APPLAUD ALL PROGRESS
Every time you see improvement, give them timely and appropriate, positive feedback.

3. BE A GRACE-GIVER
Remember your own chains, stains and pains—extend grace whenever you can.

4. CULTIVATE AN INCURABLE OPTIMISM WITHIN YOURSELF
Work hard to see the positive side of people; focus on this side during conversations.

5. GIVE THEM CHALLENGES THEY CAN RISE TO AND CONQUER
Create realistic challenges for them to apply truth, and put "wins" under their belts.

6. INVEST TIME IN SHARED EXPERIENCES
Belief in people grows as you gain shared experience; spend time together on their turf.

7. IDENTIFY WITH SIMILARITIES IN TEMPERAMENT AND STYLE
We deepen our ability to believe in mentorees when we see how alike we are.
8. GIVE THEM WHAT YOU KNOW THEY NEED, NOT DESERVE
Do what you would like others to do for you; gratitude motivates faster than guilt.

You can bank on the fact that Barnabas consistently practiced the items on this list. Why? As Emerson has said, "Our chief want is someone who will inspire us to be what we could be." Evidently it paid off in Mark's life. Later, when the Apostle Paul penned his final letter to Timothy, he "changed his tune" concerning Mark. Listen to his words: "Pick up Mark and bring him with you, for he is useful to me for service (II Timothy 4:11)." Wow! It is doubtful he could have written these words if Barnabas had not believed in and invested in Mark, years earlier.

Mentoring Keys

THE MENTORING RELATIONSHIP: *Missionary and Young, Potential Minister*

THE METHOD OF EMPOWERMENT: *Emotional support and belief; time spent; ministry model; encouragement; shared experience*

THE GOD GIVEN RESOURCES: *Ministry experiences; lots of grace; wise counsel; opportunities after his mentoree had failed*

REFLECT AND RESPOND...

1. In their first missionary journey, John Mark failed the team. Everyone fails at some point. What enables a mentor to believe in a mentoree instead of throw in the towel?

2. Why do we believe in some people we know, and not others? Be specific.

3. Barnabas gave John Mark a second chance at ministry. Has someone you know given you a "second chance" after you failed at a task? What did it do to you inside?

4. Has anyone failed you recently? What items on the list above did you practice? Which ones were more difficult to practice?

5. What is the most important observation you've made concerning Barnabas and Mark?

PAUL &

AQUILA & PRISCILLA

Acts 18:1-4, 18, Romans 16:3

In an optimal situation, Cuvier, the naturalist, was very democratic in his tastes. He loved and poured into his students regardless of who they were or where they'd been. He treated all men as equals, and would not allow others to treat him as a superior.

One day, while discussing a question in anatomy, a student interjected in his conversation, "Monsieur le baron..."

"There is no baron here," replied Cuvier. "There are only students here seeking Truth—all of us. And we only bow down to her."

This kind of attitude has kept many a mentor in a place of teachability and humility. Often these mentors see themselves as fellow "learners" and that they are merely pointing the way to their apprentices. This allows both the student and the mentor to make contributions to the process. Just ask Paul the Apostle. He struck up this kind of relationship with a couple in Greece and both of them benefited from it. Although he was clearly the mentor, he was able to receive from them, allowing for them to make their addition to the discipleship process.

Discipleship took place all through the book of Acts. Disciple-makers were taking young mentorees (or disciples) under their wings and passing on resources that would enable them to grow and reproduce. One such discipleship relationship took place between the Apostle Paul and a couple, named Aquila and Priscilla (Acts 18:1-4).

They first met in Corinth, Greece. Paul arrived there for the first time, and they met soon after his arrival. This mentoring relationship is first an illustration of *personal chemistry.* Paul found two individuals of like-mind, and matched up with them, finding maximum results due to the similarities of their lives. Notice some of the more prominent ones below:

- They shared the same religious and ethnic heritage (Jewish)
- They shared the same citizenship (Roman)
- They shared the same profession (Tent making)
- They shared the same city for a year and a half (Corinth)
- They shared the same home, for the same time period
- They shared the same passion for Jesus Christ
- They shared the same calling to serve as laborers to the Gentiles

During his one and a half years with this couple, Paul became their personal mentor. He invested time and spiritual resources in them. In turn, they gave Paul a home, food and some good fellowship and emotional refuge. So close did they become, that when Paul left Corinth for Syria—he took them with him (Acts 18:18)! They traveled together to strengthen the churches in Ephesus, Philippi and ultimately they went to Rome. Paul greets them in Romans 16:3 and says: "Greet Priscilla and Aquila, my fellow workers in Christ Jesus, who for my life risked their own necks, to whom not only do I give thanks, but also all the churches of the Gentiles..."

Those are gracious words! They were birthed out of their common experience of travel; planting churches; strengthening leaders; discipling and teaching Christians; evangelizing Hebrews in the synagogue and sharpening each other when they got time to relax and fellowship together. As in so many other biblical relationships, the mentoring happened as they experienced ministry and a common passion...together. Illustration #2: This mentor relationship is a vivid example of the proverbial "win/win." *It was one of mutual benefit!* While Paul was clearly the apostle, leader and wise "mentor" for Aquila and Priscilla, they provided needed resources for him as well. Note the mutual benefits below:

Paul Gave Aquila/Priscilla:	Aquila/Priscilla Gave Paul:
1. God-given authority and affirmation	
2. Ministry experience for their gifts	1. A home to stay in and food to eat
3. Theological insight/counsel	2. Friendship and emotional refreshment
	3. Financial and provisional support
4. Missionary opportunities	4. Able ministry on Paul's missionary team
5. Training for church leadership	5. Fellow workers to train

This relationship demonstrates that mentoring can go both ways. It doesn't have to look like the traditional "guru" who has nuggets of wisdom dribbling off of his lips, and whose protégés are only in the relationship to receive those nuggets. Mentorees have something to give to their mentors as well! Aquila and Priscilla gave Paul rich fellowship, tangible gifts, and even released him to be able to minister full time in Corinth, being willing to do the tentmaking by themselves. This is a paradigm every one of us should embrace.

Mentoring Keys

THE MENTORING RELATIONSHIP: *Apostle and Christian Workers*

THE METHOD OF EMPOWERMENT: *Opportunities to serve and travel on the mission team; leadership training; theological counsel*

THE GOD GIVEN RESOURCES: *Wisdom; ministry experience; cross cultural training; God given authority; positions of leadership*

REFLECT AND RESPOND...

1. Paul and this couple (Aquila and Priscilla) spent lots of time together. That's a benefit for any mentoring relationship. However, it appears they worked together, lived and ate together, then ministered together in the synagogue. Are there potential liabilities to having so much time together?

2. Paul both gave to and received from his mentorees. They both gave the other what was needed most by them. Can you list a relationship you have now, that provides this kind of "win/win" experience?

3. What is so beneficial to possessing good "chemistry" between mentor and mentoree? Do you have a mentor like this now? How about a mentoree?

4. Are there any pitfalls to being so much alike?

5. Someone once said that the chief gain from a "peer mentor" is accountability. What do you believe is the difference in what you gain out of a peer mentor, as opposed to a "teacher/student" mentoring relationship?

AQUILA & PRISCILLA & APOLLOS

Y ears ago, in India, the infamous leader Ghandi was board-
ing a train. As he stepped aboard the train that day, one of his shoes
slipped off and landed on the track. He was unable to retrieve it as
the train was moving. To the amazement of his companions, Ghandi
calmly took off his other shoe and threw it back along the track
close to the first.

Asked by a fellow passenger why he did so, Ghandi smiled.
"The poor man who finds the shoe lying on the track," he replied,
"will now have a pair he can use."

This is the kind of generous spirit that good mentors possess.
They are always thinking of the recipients of their resources. They
are always giving to others, and are attractive to mentorees because
they are so useful and practical.

This is the kind of generosity we find in the hearts of Aquila
and Priscilla. They had both received from Paul's mentoring, then
quickly passed on what they'd received to others.

One of the most obvious mentoring relationships recorded in
Acts is the one that emerged between Aquila, Priscilla and Apollos.
We read about their meeting and match up in Acts 18:24-28. The
couple that the Apostle Paul had invested so much time in
mentoring—was now investing their own lives in a mentoree! It
must have been rewarding for Paul to watch his mentorees turn
around and duplicate precisely what he had done with them: they
found Christians loaded with potential—and made deposits in their
lives. Such was the case with a young preacher named Apollos.

Like their own mentor, Aquila and Priscilla teach us how to
spot quality people to invest in. Apollos was already teaching and
preaching when they found him one day, in Ephesus. They quickly

discerned the signs in his life that make for a fruitful mentoree:
Apollos had:

1. **An evident gift** (He had definite spiritual gifts for ministry)
2. **An obedient life** (He was already exercising them, serving people)
3. **A hungry heart** (He was teachable and thirsty for improvement)

As in the case study of Barnabas mentoring Saul, Aquila and Priscilla took initiative, and "took him (their mentoree) aside" to interact with him. They didn't want to publicly embarrass him by correcting or exhorting him in front of everyone; they met with him in a "safe place" privately. In Acts 18:24-28, we gather three mentoring principles from Aquila and Priscilla that almost guaranteed their success. If we'll follow their model, the effectiveness of our relationships with mentorees will improve, as well.

First, they chose their mentoree well. Apollos is described in v.24-26a. Luke records nothing but positive qualities about him. In fact, we learn from the text that Apollos was not only gifted, but...

- *He was educated in mind* (Alexandria was one of the top learning centers in the world)
- *He was eloquent in speech* (He spoke well: he was both polished and bold)
- *He was excellent in religion* (He was committed to all the truth he knew)
- *He was experienced with scripture* (He knew the Word and taught it accurately)
- *He was enthusiastic in spirit* (He was zealous and fervent and served with power)

These make for a good mentoree, to say the least! Apollos was demonstrating a life that would make any mentor *long to invest their life in them,* knowing the certain return.

They communicated and challenged their mentoree well. As Aquila and Priscilla interacted with Apollos, they did so with deep wisdom and discretion. When they noticed that Apollos had only the gospel of repentance taught by John the Baptizer, they took him aside, in private, and "explained to him the Word of God more accurately" (v. 26). We have no reason to believe he felt patronized or condescended to; they must have affirmed all of the items Luke listed in his description of Apollos. It was then, however, they were able to improve the quality and accuracy of his ministry. What he needed was three "gifts:" 1) a revelation of God's grace; 2) correction and addition of the complete New Testament message and 3) trusted authorities who could turn into gracious teachers. These mentors must have given these gifts freely, because later in the text (v.27), "he helped greatly those who had believed through grace."

They commissioned their mentoree well. Finally, we see that Aquila and Priscilla didn't try to cling to their mentoree, but released him to return to his ministry (v. 27-28). What happened to Apollos when he arrived at Achaia gives us insight. We learn from Paul's letter to the Corinthians that Apollos became a leader of the church there. It is significant Luke tells us that Apollos helped those in Corinth understand "grace." The very issue that was yet unsettled in his own life when Aquila and Priscilla found him— was afterwards the descriptive phrase of his ministry. The truth his mentors shared not only changed his own life, but continued to change the lives of his mentorees, forever!

Mentoring Keys

THE MENTORING RELATIONSHIP: *Apostolic Team Members and Teacher*

THE METHOD OF EMPOWERMENT: *Observation and evaluation; biblical instruction; private discussions; affirmation/correction*

THE GOD GIVEN RESOURCES: *Biblical insight; a "grace experience;" quality time*

REFLECT AND RESPOND...

1. Aquila and Priscilla found Apollos in a synagogue, teaching— already exercising his ministry gifts. Where are the logical "ministry laboratories" today where you might find some quality mentorees, already practicing their faith?

2. If you were Apollos, what would you most appreciate about the mentoring style and substance of Aquila and Priscilla?

3. What signals does the above scripture give us that Apollos was a teachable mentoree?

4. One of the greatest gifts that Aquila and Priscilla gave to Apollos was the "release" to return to his ministry and mentoring. Did you ever have a mentor who did an excellent job "commissioning" you into ministry and spiritual reproduction? What steps did they take? How did they get you to spiritually reproduce?

PAUL
& SILAS

Acts 15:40-41, 17:10-15

Paul Villiard writes about how his family had one of the first telephones on his block, as a small boy. He remembers how he first discovered the amazing person inside that phone box, named "Information Please." There was nothing she did not know—including phone numbers in town and the correct time of the day.

Villiard recalls how he smashed his finger with a hammer as an eight year old. His mother was gone, so he had no one to cry with—until he called "Information." The voice simply asked, "Isn't your mother home?" When he replied she wasn't, "Information Please" told him to get an icepack and hold it against his hurt finger—and that he would be fine.

Later, he called "Information Please" to ask how to spell the word "fix." When she spelled it for him, he remembers calling her for questions on geography, science and math as well. All this took place in a small town in the Pacific Northwest. When he was nine years old, his family moved to Boston. He wrote, "I missed my mentor acutely...yet the memories of those conversations never really left me; I would recall the serene sense of security I had when I knew that I could call "Information Please" and get the right answer."

As an adult, Paul Villiard left for college and happened to call his sister in the Seattle area. Afterward, without really thinking, he called his "phone mentor" after years of distance. He simply asked, "Could you tell me how to spell the word 'fix'?"

There was a long pause. Then came a soft voice: "I guess that your finger must have healed by now."

Both of them laughed and couldn't believe they were talking again after all those years. He said, "So it's really still you. I wonder if you have any idea how much you meant to me during my growing up years. Thank you for talking with me."

"I wonder," she replied, "if you know how much you meant to me? I never had any children, and I actually used to look forward to your calls and your questions. Thank *you* for talking with *me!*"

This touching childhood story illustrates the mutual benefit that mentors and mentorees can receive from each other. Both of the anonymous voices had a need met from their conversations. In the same way, Paul and Silas entered into a mentoring relationship in the book of Acts that became a "win/win" situation for both of them. Silas met needs in the Apostle's life, as well as vice versa. Both contributed to the other.

The Apostle Paul was involved in several of the mentoring relationships written up in the New Testament. He believed in the "apprentice" system of training ministers, and always seemed to need their help in his church planting efforts. Such was the case when he challenged Silas to join his ministry team in Acts 15:40-41.

The mentoring story of Paul and Silas is more a story of a "model mentoree" or protégé, than it is of a perfect mentor. Doubtless, Paul poured his life into Silas (as his mentor), but we never get the details of that life-investment. What we do read in Acts 15 and 17 is about an active young man who was noticed by Paul as having "massive" potential, and was ready to join him on his next mission trip. In Acts 15:40-41 and Acts 17:10-15 we read of their introduction, and subsequent mentoring relationship. I believe we can make five helpful observations (and applications) on Silas, as a model mentoree for Paul:

1. HE WAS AVAILABLE TO PAUL (15:34)

This had to do with his position and proximity. Silas was not from Antioch, where we first read about him. However, he decides to stay on there, due to ministry and mentoring opportunities. The scripture says "it seemed good to Silas to remain there." He postured himself in the right position to both give and receive ministry.

He stayed nearby.

2. HE WAS CHOSEN BY PAUL (15:40)

This had to do with his potential and participation. Silas had proven he possessed ministry savvy and demonstrated his gifts to the folks at Antioch, an unfamiliar place to him. His mentor saw his raw potential because he had taken the risk of participating in serving the church. He was ready to be part of the team.

3. HE WAS USEFUL TO PAUL (15:41)

This had to do with his prophetic and pastoral abilities. In 15:32 Luke calls him a prophet, and in verse 41 we read that he went with Paul "strengthening the churches" in Syria and Cilicia. He used his gifts, not merely to gain others' attention, but to actually bear fruit and meet needs in those areas.

4. HE WAS TRUSTWORTHY FOR PAUL (17:14)

This had to do with his perspective and principled life. Silas exhibited a sense of deep responsibility for Paul's ministry. So much so, that Paul left him and Timothy in Berea to give leadership to the new Christians while he moved on to Athens. Silas did not merely do well in the presence of his mentor, but was able to do it *on his own,* when necessary.

5. HE WAS COMPATIBLE WITH PAUL (17:15)

This had to do with his passion and partnership qualities. In verse 15 Paul sends a command to Silas and Timothy to "come to him with all speed." They were needed, not so much because Paul couldn't preach alone, but because Silas' gifts and passion so fit and complimented his mentor's. There was synergy; they were better working with each other. Silas seemed to complete Paul's ministry.

If only each of us could incarnate these qualities with our mentors, AND find mentorees who fit us as well, like a "hand and a glove." Interestingly, Silas was chosen when Paul and Barnabas couldn't agree on John Mark's role on the team. As it turned out, both Paul and Barnabas ended up with suitable mentorees, and went their separate ways: Barnabas become Mark's mentor; Paul became Silas' mentor. God has a way of "multiplying" the Kingdom even through strife!

Mentoring Keys

THE MENTORING RELATIONSHIP: *Apostle and Prophet*

THE METHOD OF EMPOWERMENT: *On-the-job training; clear ministry tasks; belief in him (he was hand-picked)*

THE GOD GIVEN RESOURCES: *Credibility; ministry authority and experience; wisdom and direction; growth opportunities*

REFLECT AND RESPOND...

1. Silas was personally chosen by the Apostle Paul to travel with him. What kinds of emotional responses does "being chosen" by an authority figure provoke in you?

2. Paul observed Silas in action, and determined he would make a good mentoree and team member. What if a potential mentor were to observe YOU in action. What kind of judgment would they render? Would you be seen as a good "investment" for a mentor?

3. Silas demonstrated qualities that make for a good mentoree, especially for the one who is a "mentor/coach." Which of these qualities (above) do you incarnate naturally?

4. What do you need to work on most (or deliberately apply yourself to) as a mentoree? As a mentor? What should be your number one prayer request in this area?

5. What is the most important lesson you learned from Paul and Silas?

PAUL
&TIMOTHY

Acts 16:1-3, I Timothy 1:1-3, 18-19, II Timothy 1:1-6, 4:1-5

Dawson Trotman, the founder of The Navigators, is a beautiful example of spiritual multiplication. Early in his ministry, a young sailor approached him and asked him to help him grow. "Daws" clarified that what the sailor was really asking for was to be discipled or mentored. He then agreed to do it, over the next several months. During that experience, this sailor's life was so dramatically changed, that he brought a buddy of his to Trotman and requested that Daws disciple him as well. The reply startled the sailors: "Absolutely not." Then Daws went on to say, "If your friend is going to be discipled, it will be you who does it." So, the two of them connected in a discipleship relationship. Upon their completion, the chain continued. Both went out and found someone else in whom they could invest their lives. This happened again and again and again on that ship.

What makes this story so intriguing is that it literally transformed the atmosphere of the ship. Posters came down in their rooms; cursing became rare. The Commanding Officers wondered what was going on. Eventually, the F.B.I. was called to investigate. Some thought a cult had broken out. Others simply questioned the odd behavior of what was once a "normal" group of sailors. Clearly things were different. What's more, once the FBI began to investigate, it took them six months to sift through all the men who had been discipled in order to find "Daws"—the one who had started the whole thing. The "web" of disciples was thick and transforming.

This powerful account is an illustration of what Paul commanded Timothy to do: take the truths that he had given him and entrust them to faithful men who would teach others also. Timothy became the classic "disciple" who reproduced what Paul had given him, over and over again.

When we think of ministry/mentoring in the New Testament—we usually think of the Apostle Paul, first. And, when we think of the classic mentoring match-up from his life—we usually think of young Timothy. Paul called Timothy "my son in the faith."

Why did Paul feel so devoted to this young disciple? In Philippians 2:20 he writes that he knew of no one who had such a kindred spirit for people as Timothy did. In this young mentoree, Paul saw a youthful version of himself. Consequently, he poured himself into Timothy—mentoring him in Lystra, taking him on mission trips, letting him preach, leaving him to pastor emerging churches, writing instructional letters to him, etc. There wasn't anything Paul wouldn't do for this young protégé.

Their story begins in Acts 16:1-3, when Paul first challenges Timothy to become his apprentice. Below are some of the major *principles* that Paul employed while selecting and training this mentoree. Read them over and see if you can make application to your own life:

The Principle of Purposeful Pursuit. Paul was pro-active in locating a disciple he could train. He had been to Lystra, Timothy's home town, before, and knew he was there. He insisted that his team return again. He was determined to go after Timothy and challenge him to be his mentoree, knowing the kind of man he was. His antennas were always up.

The Principle of Proven Potential. Paul did his homework on Timothy. He knew he was a diamond in the rough. He had watched Timothy prove himself in his own hometown while growing up. He knew his family, his potential and the spiritual "stock" he'd come from.

The Principle of Practical Patience. Paul was a patient man when it came to selecting and mentoring potential ministers. He was careful not to act prematurely, and even advised: "lay hands on no man suddenly." He felt his team had acted too quickly in letting John Mark travel with them (Acts 12:25). He didn't want to pick fruit too early.

The Principle of the Participatory Process. Paul recognized that he (as a mentor) was one participant in a long process of contributors in Timothy's life. In II Timothy 1:5 he reminded his mentoree of other mentors in his life: his mother and grandmother. Timothy had a strong heritage before Paul came along. Paul simply played his role in the process.

The Principle of Passion and Pricetags. Paul wrote to his mentoree in II Timothy 2:2-3 and said: "The things which you have heard from me...these entrust to faithful men, who will be able to teach others also. Suffer hardship with me, as a good soldier of Christ Jesus." The two verses go together. Spiritual reproduction means hardship. Paul outlined four generations of "disciples" in verse two above, but it all began with tremendous pain! Paul found Timothy in Lystra—but was stoned and left for dead! What a price he paid. He recovered, then went right back into the city—to get Timothy. This kind of *passion* for spiritual reproduction is the only ingredient that will enable you to face such hardship.

Quite possibly, Timothy was Paul's most prized "trophy" as a mentoree. He responded to all of his mentor's instruction and example. No wonder Paul freely invested so much in him. He was Paul's legacy, left to serve with Paul's thumbprint on his back.

Mentoring Keys

THE MENTORING RELATIONSHIP: *Apostle and Disciple/ Apprentice*

THE METHOD OF EMPOWERMENT: *Shared experience; instruction; ministry opportunities; ministry-model to emulate; parental nurture*

THE GOD GIVEN RESOURCES: *Tools for ministry; epistles; leadership training and fellow-leaders to work with; guidelines to follow for life*

REFLECT AND RESPOND...

1. Paul had his eye on Timothy well before he challenged him to be his apprentice. Based on the scriptures above, what do you suppose Paul *saw* in him that was so attractive?

2. What did Paul do to demonstrate his commitment to invest in Timothy? What similar things can we do today, that exhibits our commitment to our mentoree/mentor?

3. Paul knew that he merely played one of several mentoring roles in Timothy's life. How do we discern what *our role* is, as we consider investing in a mentoree? Do you know what kind of contribution you can make in someone's life?

4. One of Paul's prime teaching tools was the "shared ministry experience." He took Timothy with him on apostolic, church planting trips across Asia. What might be some strategic "experiences" you could share with someone today, as teaching tools?

5. Paul reproduced his life in Timothy, then challenged him to do so with others (II Timothy 2:2). How can we insure that our mentorees are going to reproduce what we have invested in them?

PAUL
&Titus

Titus 1:1-5, Galatians 2:1-5, II Corinthians 7:13-16

Stephen Covey, best selling author of *Seven Habits of Highly Effective People*, recalls his childhood, and how his parents belief in him empowered him to reach his potential: "My parents were just constantly affirming me in everything that I did. Late at night I'd wake up and hear my mother talking over my bed, saying, 'You're going to do great on this test. You can do anything you want."

"I never did any drinking at all, or smoking, but I had some friends who did and we went on a trip one time and came home, and they had a fifth. They couldn't take it to their home, because they were in trouble with their parents, so I took that fifth—I've never told anyone this—and I put that fifth right in the center of my dresser. My parents never asked a question, never said a thing about it, because they knew I wasn't going to do anything with it. It was symbolic of their affirmation."

This same kind of empowerment occurred between Paul and Titus. The apostle believed in Titus, and could trust him with the toughest of ministry assignments. It was affirming to Titus when Paul wrote of his sincere faith in him, yet it was also affirming just to have Paul entrust a difficult situation to him and never ask a question or raise a concern.

Paul's mentoring relationship to Titus often gets lost in the shadows of I and II Timothy or the mentorees listed in the book of Acts. Titus' name never occurs in Acts and appears in only three of Paul's other letters, II Corinthians, Galatians, and II Timothy.

However, the little information we have indicates that Titus became one of Paul's closest and most trusted apprentices and colleagues. In Titus 1:4 Paul calls him his "true son in the faith." In

II Corinthians 8:16-17 Titus is described as having the same "earnestness" that Paul had for the people and even went to Corinth to appeal to them *on his own initiative.* Clearly, these two men were "cut out of the same cloth." This like-mindedness (for the people), and similar-giftedness (apostolic) led to a marvelous match-up for Paul, the mentor and Titus, his mentoree. How much of the qualities we see in Titus were passed on by Paul, we may never know. However, both men by the conclusion of their lives, possessed the attributes that make for great spiritual pioneers:

1. *Initiative*   3. *Integrity*
2. *Influence*   4. *Industry*

Paul and Titus could be described as *"peer mentors"* for each other due to their similarity. They both had something to add to the other's life and ministry, and assumed that role. Our focus here, however, will be on Titus, as a true "protégé" of Paul. Paul certainly chose his men well, and further—reproduced qualities in them that could sustain his influence (when he left them in churches), long after he had gone. The following descriptive terms are the ones we can spot in Titus, as Paul's mentoree. Again, they were either present when Paul found him (a tribute to Paul's selection), or they were passed on to him by Paul (a tribute to his disciple-making abilities). Here is a character sketch of the mentoree, Titus:

HE WAS A TRUSTED SON

When Paul traveled to Jerusalem to fight for his approach to salvation by grace through faith alone, he took Titus with him. He was his prime exhibit of a Gentile convert worthy of full acceptance in the church, apart from the ritual of circumcision. Paul must have known the kind of impression his son/protégé would make on the other apostles and elders. Although Titus was a Greek, he proved himself to be a disciple and a colleague. Paul's choice of Titus on the momentous occasion was vindicated; Titus was accepted.

HE WAS A TROUBLE SHOOTER

Like Paul, Titus was a tough, bottom line decision maker and trouble shooter. The fact that he was on special assignment for Paul in a very tough place like Crete speaks powerfully about Paul's regard for Titus as a competent leader and pastor, who could solve problems well (Titus 1:5). We can assume from the reference in II Corinthians that Titus actually became Paul's most valuable "trouble shooter." The picture we get of him from the pen of Paul is not unlike that of a secretary of state being sent again and again to troubled places on missions of diplomacy.

HE WAS A TASK-ORIENTED SPECIALIST

Paul sent Titus on a number of assignments that required a specialist in diplomacy and tact. He was sent to Corinth to collect an offering for the needy in Jerusalem (II Corinth. 8:1-6, 16-24). On another occasion, Paul sent him back to Corinth to straighten out some messy situations and to confront some of Paul's opponents there. Finally, we know that Paul had sent Titus to Crete to finish what he'd started and to establish leaders there (Titus 1:4-5). No doubt, Titus played a peer role of ambassador for Paul bringing closure to unfinished business.

HE WAS A TEACHABLE SERVANT

Finally, although Titus was a strong leader he demonstrated himself to be a meek and willing learner under the tutelage of Paul. He remained subordinate to Paul and we have no record of his questioning Paul's authority in his life. He appears to be a prime example of a "servant leader." He seemed to be successful on each endeavor Paul sent him and became invaluable in reaching the church in Asia-minor, since he was a Gentile himself.

Mentoring Keys

THE MENTORING RELATIONSHIP: *Apostle and Pastoral Colleague*

THE METHOD OF EMPOWERMENT: *Wisdom and instruction; ministry opportunities; affirmation*

Mentoring Keys continued...

THE GOD GIVEN RESOURCES: *Valuable leadership experience*

REFLECT AND RESPOND...

1. One of the terms used above to describe Paul and Titus was: "peer mentors." This means that both served to invest themselves and their resources in the other. Do you have a "peer mentor" or accountability partner that you look to regularly? What are the benefits?

2. Titus clearly had some similar leadership gifts to Paul. From your study of Titus, what specific additions do you think he made to Paul's ministry? What did he seem to do better than Paul?

3. Is locating a "peer mentor" easier for you than finding a mentor or mentoree, in the traditional sense? Why or why not?

4. What is the most important lesson you have learned from Paul and Titus?

PAUL
& ONESIMUS
Philemon 1:10-16

Years ago I remember hearing a report about a near tragedy that struck a summer youth camp. A man risked his life by swimming through a treacherous riptide to save a young man being swept out to sea. After the boy recovered from the harrowing experience, he summoned the man to express his gratitude: "Thank you for saving my life!"

The man looked into the boy's eyes and gently but firmly responded: "It's okay, kid. Just make sure you live a life that was worth saving."

Those words are compelling...and almost haunting. They remind me of Jesus' words to the woman caught in adultery: "Neither do I condemn you—go and sin no more." There was an extension of grace, but not without an exhortation to a higher level of living. Such was the challenge of the Apostle Paul to a young man named Onesimus.

The story of Onesimus is a tale of miraculous intervention. He was a runaway slave, who, at one time belonged to Philemon, a convert of the Apostle Paul. He connected with Paul, himself, at a later date as a refugee far from home. It was at this point that a mentoring relationship began between the two of them.

How did Onesimus meet Paul? Perhaps he had heard him personally in Ephesus in the company of his master Philemon. Or, perhaps he had seen such a transformation in his master after Philemon's conversion that curiosity drove him to inquire about the source of this "new religion" making such a big difference in the house where he served. We can assume that there was some introduction—because Onesimus specifically sought out Paul when he arrived in Rome. Paul was in prison—but evidently, so was

Onesimus in his own heart of hearts. He had run away from his responsibility to Philemon (as a slave), seeking freedom in the capitol of the empire. He must have figured he'd find real life there, out from under the bondage of slavery. But once he "hit bottom" on his own, and the freedom for which he had risked his life did not give him the meaning he sought, he turned to Paul in Rome. Interestingly, this slave was now seeking the counsel of a prison inmate! As Paul mentored him into the Kingdom, Onesimus began to submit to Paul—this time a servant of his own free will. As a mentor, Paul played three crucial roles in his life. I have outlined these roles below. After surveying them, you will likely agree it was no wonder that this slave, Onesimus, was so willing to do the bidding of his newfound mentor.

PAUL BECAME HIS DELIVERER. Once he found Paul in a Roman prison, Onesimus also found the salvation that had so changed his master, Philemon. Paul led him to Christ while Onesimus visited him in prison. He had come to seek refuge in Paul, and Paul led him to the ultimate Refuge, Jesus Christ (v. 10). It was then that Onesimus experienced *true freedom.* Paul had led him to it, ironically, while he was in chains. Here he was—now converted through the ministry of the same man by whom his master had been converted; by the same dear friend of the master from whom he had escaped.

PAUL BECAME HIS DISCIPLER. The first agenda item on Paul's list for Onesimus was to disciple and develop him as a responsible man of God. Onesimus didn't have to stick around for this—but he did. He deliberately stayed with Paul in prison to get the mentoring experience; the spiritual parenting he so desperately needed. Paul taught him the fundamentals. He became his "spiritual director" or accountant who gave him insight as to what his next steps ought to be. Although Paul would have loved to have kept Onesimus with him in prison (v.13), he encouraged this slave to do what was right and return to his master, now as a "brother in the Lord." Paul knew that his (personal) loss, was a gain for the Kingdom (v.14-16).

PAUL BECAME HIS DEFENDER. Paul knew that after he'd mentored Onesimus for a season, he would need to send him back to his master, and let Philemon decide the fate of this runaway slave. In doing so, Paul determined he would be the chief advocate and defender of Onesimus. Paul calls him his son (v.10); he tells Philemon that he is useful to both of them (v.11); he asks Philemon to receive Onesimus as he would him (v.17); and he then communicates that if Onesimus owes him anything, to put it on his account (v.18). Although he could have dictated to Philemon how to respond (v.19), Paul would not presume on Philemon's generosity. He would not force an expression of love. He knew love could work fully only in the context of freedom. Hence, Paul made the appeal.

Onesimus was an unlikely "mentoree" and Paul was in an unlikely place to do any mentoring. However, the providence of God brought these brothers together, and have forever left a model for us, as we confront difficult mentoring situations.

Mentoring Keys

THE MENTORING RELATIONSHIP: *Apostle (in prison) and Runaway Slave*

THE METHOD OF EMPOWERMENT: *Time; wise counsel; future direction*

THE GOD GIVEN RESOURCES: *Credibility with Philemon; friendship; belief in him*

REFLECT AND RESPOND...

1. When Onesimus reached Paul in prison, he must have been desperate. Have you ever sought out a mentor in a desperate situation? How does this affect your "teachability?"

2. Onesimus paid a high price to get time with Paul: he spent time with him in prison. What is the highest price you've ever paid to gain some wise counsel from a mentor?

3. When Paul wrote his epistle to Philemon, he defended Onesimus as a brother, over and over again. What does this kind of advocacy do to a mentoree? How do you suppose Onesimus (a former slave) felt returning to Philemon with these words in print?

4. Paul clearly spoke to his mentoree about responsibility. He then sent him home to do what was right. What is the most difficult lesson a mentor has ever taught you?

5. What is the most significant lesson you can learn from this delicate situation?

PAUL
& PHILEMON

Philemon 1:17-21

In the early 19th century, a young man in London aspired to be a writer. But everything seemed to be against him. He had never been able to attend school more than four years. His father had been thrown in jail because he couldn't pay his debts, and this young man often knew the pangs of hunger. Finally, he got a job pasting labels on bottles in a rat-infested warehouse, and he slept at night in a dismal attic room with two other boys. He had so little confidence in his ability to write that he sneaked out and mailed his first manuscript in the dead of night so nobody would laugh at him. Story after story was refused. Finally the great day came when one was accepted. True, he wasn't paid for it, but one editor had praised and complimented him. One editor had given him recognition. He was so thrilled that he wandered aimlessly around the streets with tears rolling down his cheeks.

The praise and affirmation that he received through getting one story in print changed his whole life. If it hadn't been for that encouragement, he might have spent his entire life working in rat-infested factories. You may have heard of that boy. His name is Charles Dickens.

Interestingly, one of Dickens' greatest pieces was called, *Great Expectations.* It was this kind of praise and high expectation that enabled him to perform beyond his wildest imaginations. People tend to rise to the level of others' expectations. And it is this principle that Paul the Apostle employed when he addressed a friend named Philemon, about the difficult issue of his runaway slave, Onesimus.

On the heels of Paul's encounter with Onesimus, in the Roman prison, he decides to do a little mentoring through the mail to his close friend and convert, Philemon. Paul and Philemon had likely met when both were visiting Ephesus, a port city. Paul had led him to the Lord and discipled him to the point that Philemon had a church meeting in his home in Colosse. Indeed, he had bought into the Christian lifestyle, "hook, line and sinker."

Philemon and Paul had a heavy issue to discuss, however, which became the theme of this epistle. It was the sticky subject of Onesimus' sudden departure from his responsibilities as Philemon's slave. He had run away, and Paul felt compelled to influence Philemon to receive him back, *as a brother*, with no penalties (v.17-18). Clearly, this was asking a lot of Philemon. Would he be angry or upset? Would he even speak to Paul after discovering Paul had helped Onesimus? Paul was faced with the necessary but undesirable task of *confrontation*. He needed to speak difficult words into the life of his mentoree, Philemon.

Fortunately, Paul was a master mentor when it came to handling conflict. He seemed to understand the fundamental truths about conflict that make it less stressful:

- **Conflict is Natural** (It is going to occur simply because of our human differences.)
- **Conflict is Neutral** (It is neither destructive or constructive in itself.)
- **Conflict is Normal** (It happens to all of us; none of us are alone in facing it.)

The following represents how Paul chose to approach this difficult time with his mentoree, Philemon. Notice his clear steps to conflict management as they are outlined below...

1. COMPLIMENT (v.4-7)

His first item of business was to compliment and affirm his mentoree. His focus was on the positive qualities that first drew him to Philemon. When we begin this way, we start on the right footing. This is commonly called the "101% Principle:" Find the 1% you agree on or can appreciate, and give it 100% of your attention.

2. COMPROMISE (v.8-13)

Next, Paul makes an appeal to Philemon. He brings up the subject in question and even concedes that Onesimus at one time was useless to him. He meets Philemon on his turf. We, too, must admit early that we're willing to assume some responsibility for the conflict, recognizing differences in motivation, style and perspective. We must meet them halfway.

3. CHOICE (v.14)

At this point, Paul communicates that he'll not demand a particular response. He wants to proceed only with Philemon's consent, and he presents him with a choice. Like Paul, we must be clear in laying out the decision in front of both parties. We can flee it, fight it or face it. Do all you can to maintain the relationship *and* the goals you've agreed to pursue.

4. CHALLENGE (v.15-20)

Paul then extends a clear challenge to Philemon. He makes a case for why they ought to do what's best for Onesimus, and presents that option as a "win/win." As we come to this part of the confrontation, we must remember: *it's more important to win the soul than the argument.* Lay out good perimeters and boundaries you feel are appropriate for success.

5. CONFIDENCE (v.21)

Finally, Paul concludes by expressing his sincere confidence in Philemon to do even more than what he was asking! We must learn this art of communicating confidence in them as a person and in their judgment. Tell them you trust them to make the right decision and that no personal differences will prevent you from loving them.

Every mentoring relationship encounters some degree of conflict, if for no other reason than our mere human differences. Mentoring is a little like marriage. You fall in love with the other person's *strengths* but must live with their *weaknesses.* We must learn from Paul, the mentor, and develop our ability to resolve tough issues, so that our mentorees gain the "tools" (themselves) to reproduce healthy relationships.

Mentoring Keys

THE MENTORING RELATIONSHIP: *Apostle and Convert/ Comrade*

THE METHOD OF EMPOWERMENT: *A personal letter; lots of warmth and love*

THE GOD GIVEN RESOURCES: *Affirmation; wise counsel and direction in a decision making process; belief in him*

REFLECT AND RESPOND...

1. Paul seemed to have no problem facing tough, relational conflict. Is it difficult for you? What do you wrestle most with, when it comes to confronting someone?

2. Which of his steps listed above do you believe you do best? Which are your weak ones that need improvement? What steps could you take to improve yourself?

3. Are you facing a person or problem that needs to be confronted now? What will you do and when? What can you learn from Paul's methods of conflict management?

4. Paul had obviously "earned" his right to speak the way he did to Philemon (v.8, 17-19). Comment on how personal investment in your mentoree can pay off when it comes time to confront them on an issue.

5. What one truth did you benefit from the most in this mentoring relationship?

PAUL & JULIUS

Acts 27

The fastest way to earn the right to influence someone is to crawl into the trenches they are in, and experience their difficulties with them. Credibility increases with shared experience.

Tracy was just five years old when she asked her dad if she could play at a friend's house. Her father told her she could as long as she was home by six o'clock for dinner.

Unfortunately, when six o'clock rolled around Tracy was no where to be found. Her dad was a bit angry with her, but determined to wait and speak with her when she did get around to returning home. After about twenty five minutes, Tracy opened the front door. Inquisitive about her tardiness, her father asked where she'd been.

"I'm sorry I'm late, dad," she responded, "but my friend's doll broke right when I was supposed to leave for home."

"Oh, I see," her dad said. "And I suppose you were helping her fix it?"

"No," replied Tracy. "I was helping her cry."

Somehow, little Tracy understood at least part of this principle. Leadership is relationship; and relationship means we're to rejoice with those who rejoice, and weep with those who weep. When we do this, we begin to earn the right to speak into their life. There is no greater demonstration of this principle than in Acts 27 when Paul boards a ship and begins to meet and relate to Julius and his crew—during their trip to Rome, Italy.

Paul's sea voyage to Rome was filled with adventure, dangers, thrills and...at least one mentoring experience on board between the Apostle Paul, (an inmate on board the ship), and Julius, the centurion in charge of the prisoners.

As horrific storms began to assail the ship, Paul warned Julius and the crew not to proceed. At this point, however, Paul had not yet earned a place of influence in his relationship with the centurion; Julius believed the helmsman more than he did Paul (v.11). It was during the trip itself that Paul won—not only the right to *befriend* Julius—but to *influence him as well.* In one very real sense, Paul became a "mentor" for this centurion, in route to their destination. What's more, he did so by *earning* his way into the hearts of both Julius and the sailors by demonstrating his sheer leadership ability. The following is a survey of how Paul gained this influential position, as an inmate on board the ship:

1. He built trust (v.3). Even though Paul was a prisoner, Julius treated him with kindness, and trusted him, due to his track record and his ministry reputation. He knew the first step is always to develop a level of trust with the one you hope to influence.

2. He took initiative (v.9). In spite of the fact that he had no human authority to step in and advise the centurion or his crew, Paul asserted himself and gave wise counsel to them. He knew that it was their lives that hung in the balance—he couldn't wait for an invitation!

3. He possessed good judgment (v.10). Paul desperately wanted to reach Rome, but not at the expense of the ship's cargo and passengers. He didn't let his personal ambitions cloud his judgment of the situation. He gave them wise counsel, even though they ignored it.

4. He spoke with authority (v.21). Paul reminded the men that they should have listened to him earlier, when he warned them not to sail from Crete. Everyone had gone for days without food, yet Paul still stood tall in the midst of them, and spoke with divine authority.

5. He strengthened others (v.22). After this "I told you so" introduction, Paul went on to encourage the crew, and inform them that no one would lose their life. He knew the necessity of strengthening the heart of Julius and the men who had to work the decks.

6. He was optimistic and enthusiastic (v.24-25). He never loses his contagious optimism about God's sovereignty over the situation. He gives divine and specific direction to the crew and reminds them boldly that it was God who had spoken these things to him.

7. He didn't compromise with absolutes (v.26-32). After the positive news about God sparing their lives, he adds the hard truth about how they must run aground on an island. When the crew wants to escape this fate, Paul confronts them, sharing that unless they follow God's direction in detail—their lives would not be spared.

8. He focused on objectives not obstacles (v.33-34). When the men were famished but still determined to save the food, Paul exhorts them to eat, assuring them of their certain destination, and that "none of them would perish." He fixed his eyes on the goal.

9. He led them by example (v.35). After this exhortation, he provides the model of his own faith, by taking the food, giving thanks to God and eating. He knew it was one thing to *tell* them what to do, and quite another to *show* them. He modeled obedience to God.

After practicing the above list of leadership principles, Paul had not only saved the lives of the men on the ship, but had clearly earned the right to lead them. Julius was ready to listen and heed his words; Paul had become the central counselor and primary influencer of Julius *as a prisoner*, even though Julius possessed the title and position of leader. He demonstrated that *leadership is not about titles or positions—but about gaining the right to influence.* In other words, it is not an *automatic privilege* but an *earned right.*

Mentoring Keys

THE MENTORING RELATIONSHIP: *Prison Inmate and Centurion*

THE METHOD OF EMPOWERMENT: *See the above list of leadership principles and practices*

THE GOD GIVEN RESOURCES: *Divine guidance and protection; enabled mentoree to achieve goals; modeled godly lifestyle and leadership*

REFLECT AND RESPOND...

1. From the principles and practices listed above, which are most natural for you? Which of them are most difficult?

2. Can you spot any other mentoring/leadership qualities that Paul exhibited in Acts 27, in addition to the ones listed above?

3. The irony of this story is, of course, that a prisoner began to influence the decisions of a Centurion. What lessons does this teach you about leadership and relationships?

4. Have you ever earned your right to lead someone who (initially) didn't want to be led? How did you do it?

JESUS
& THE TWELVE

A Summary of Matthew, Mark, Luke & John

Friday night promised to be an evening to remember for Tommy and his family. Every now and then, his dad would plan a "family night" where the whole family would spend time together playing games and laughing together in the den. Dad had planned some extra surprises for them on this particular night.

Unfortunately, earlier in the day, Tommy had misbehaved terribly. He had disobeyed, and his attitude was miserable. When his mother and father discussed the issue, he knew he was in trouble. His dad was a strict disciplinarian. Tommy was summoned by his father, and reprimanded; then—he heard the words he dreaded most: "You will not be able to do the "fun stuff" with the rest of the family tonight. You must go to your room."

Later, in bed, Tommy's thoughts of his behavior began to bother him. He couldn't remember ever having felt more alone or alienated. He began to cry. Then he heard a noise on the stairs. Footsteps came closer to his room. His door opened and his father came in. Closing the door, he came over to Tommy's bed and said, "I love you, son—and I've come to spend the night with you."

What a vivid illustration of Jesus, and his incarnation. He didn't shout his orders from heaven, but came to live with us in our miserable state, and "mentored us from below."

Clearly, no one embodied these mentoring principles better than Jesus, Himself. That is why we have saved the best "biblical model/mentor" until last. A number of wonderful books have been written about the methodology Jesus employed as he trained or discipled the twelve during His three and a half year ministry. What I believe would be helpful here is to simply distill the "factors" written up in the Gospels that made Jesus' mentoring ministry so effective. He was the Master, and He mentored imperfect humans just like you and me with absolute perfection. Their response was not always perfect—but that is not in the mentor's control. Jesus did everything a mentor can do to enable those disciples to flourish in their personal lives and ministry. He left the rest in the hands of God's Spirit.

The following is a list of *twelve factors* our Lord included in His mentoring ministry. His primary ministry on earth, according to His prayer in John 17, was to invest in these men, so that they could reproduce spiritually. This should be our primary ministry objective as well. While we all may have specific gifts to accomplish some particular ministry in our church—we should *all* be mentoring (spiritually multiplying) as we perform our tasks. Here is how Jesus did it. Note the following principles and passages...

1. INITIATIVE (Luke 6:12-13)
Jesus didn't wait for mentorees to approach Him. He was determined to leave His legacy behind through mentoring people. He prayed all night, then selected them.

2. PROXIMITY (Mark 3:14, Luke 8:1)
Jesus employed the "with him" principle. Much of His mentoring was done through the disciples merely observing His life; they were walking alongside of Him with each step.

3. FRIENDSHIP (John 15:15)
Jesus called His mentorees His "friends." It is difficult to mentor someone if you don't enjoy them as friends. He demonstrated this through his love, time and transparency.

4. EXAMPLE (John 13:15)
Jesus deliberately gave the disciples His life as an example to watch. He knew they would learn faster if He would *show* them not just *tell* them. He taught with His life.

5. COMMITMENT (John 13:1, Matthew 16:24)
Jesus both committed Himself to His relationship with the twelve, *and* asked for this same commitment from them. Mentoring doesn't work without mutual commitment.

6. RESPONSIBILITY (Mark 6:7)

Jesus soon transferred the responsibility He felt for advancing God's Kingdom to His mentorees. He gave them all ownership of the ministry through delegation and authority.

7. KNOWLEDGE (Luke 8:9-10)

Jesus taught and discussed hundreds of issues with the twelve. While His mentoring was so much more than "words," it did, indeed, involve careful instruction on His part.

8. TRUST (Matthew 10:1-8, Luke 10:1-16)

Jesus gave one of His greatest gifts to the disciples when he exhibited trust in them. He trusted them enough to give them a part in His ministry. He sent them out—in His name.

9. EVALUATION (Luke 10:17-20)

Jesus also performed the related task of assessment and evaluation. Once He trusted them with tasks, He knew they would need objective accountability on their performance.

10. GOAL (Matthew 4:19, John 4:35)

Jesus, from the very beginning, kept His goal before the mentorees: that they would be making disciples one day, themselves. He even made this part of His invitation to them.

11. POWER (John 20:22, Acts 1:8)

Jesus made sure to "empower" His mentorees before launching them into their ministry. At the close of His ministry, He ensured that the Holy Spirit was upon them in power!

12. LAUNCH (Matthew 28:18-20)

Jesus initiated one final contact and gave one final challenge to His mentorees: that they duplicate what He had just done with them! The mentorees must become mentors.

The beautiful part about these factors is that every one of us today can apply them. They are transferrable concepts and principles, that anyone, in any generation, in any location could practice. God, may you implement them through us, as we mentor others!

Mentoring Keys

THE MENTORING RELATIONSHIP: *Master and Disciples (Apprentices)*

THE METHOD OF EMPOWERMENT: *See the "factors" listed above*

THE GOD GIVEN RESOURCES: *A perfect model to follow; the empowerment of the Holy Spirit; on-the-job training; clear direction/wisdom*

REFLECT AND RESPOND...

1. Why do you suppose Jesus invested so much in the twelve disciples when He could've focused on reaching the "masses" as the divine Son of God?

2. One of the best methods for summarizing Jesus' mentoring ministry is to use the word "IDEA" as an acronym. The following is JESUS' IDEA for mentoring:

    I - INSTRUCTION...in a life related context.

    D - DEMONSTRATION...in a life related context.

    E - EXPERIENCE...in a life related context.

    A - ACCOUNTABILITY...in a life related context.

Have you ever had a mentor that gave you all four of these gifts? Which ones are you providing for someone else right now? Which one do you need to improve upon?

3. From the list of "Twelve Factors" above, which ones do you benefit from most, as a mentoree? Which of them do you perform best, as a mentor? How can you improve?

ANSWERING
THE CALL

The media has given us some beautiful portraits of "mentors" over the last several years. One such portrait came from the 1992 Summer Olympic games, held in Barcelona, Spain. Derrick Redman, an athlete from England had qualified to compete in the 440 meter event despite that fact that he'd had 22 surgeries on his Achilles heel. It was a miracle to some that he was even able to run again, not to mention qualify for the Olympics.

It was at this event, however, that tragedy struck. Somewhere midway through the race, Derrick Redman pulled up short. He had pulled a hamstring, and injured his Achilles tendon again. At least one of the cameras stayed glued to this athlete, as he limped slowly forward, wincing in pain. He could barely stay on his feet. His hopes of winning were dashed; and while he wanted desperately to finish the race—even this looked impossible. It was all over for Derrick Redman.

Enter, his mentor. Sitting in the second row from the top, in the stands—was Jim Redman, Derrick's father. He could not imagine doing anything else but get involved. He pushed his way past the huge crowd separating him from the track. He persistently moved toward the gate and pushed through the security guards, who were not able to keep this man from his mentoree. Jim had been Derrick's biggest "fan" through the years, and this move was the only logical one, for him. Quickly, the cameras focused on this "intruder" running toward the pitiful athlete from the UK. Jim put his arm around his son, and the two exchanged words. In tears, Derrick fell into his father's arms—and then, Jim did what all great mentors do for their mentorees. Jim lifted Derrick up, put his son's arm around his own shoulder—and the two finished the race together.

I remember watching this scene with tears in my eyes. I had not expected to observe such an act of love that day; to receive such a clear "snapshot" of someone investing in the life of another. I can remember the crowd applauding for the two of them as they finished the race (arm in arm), as loudly as they did the winner of the race, that day. Whether he knew it or not, Jim Redman gave the world a picture of a mentor: one who picks up the life of another, and says, "I'm going to help you finish your race, well."

THE DIFFERENCE A MENTOR MAKES...

There's something different about the words of a mentor. They mean more to a mentoree than do the words of someone else. They may not be *different* words of counsel or advice than might come from another—but they are, indeed, different. The same is true concerning the deeds of a mentor, or a gift given by a mentor, or an experience shared with a mentor, or a book loaned by a mentor. The reason for this is simple. They are birthed from a *committed relationship.* Both the mentoree and the mentor have something at stake in the outcome of the life of the other. This commitment gives every act, word and resource exchanged a deeper meaning.

If we truly believe this, then the issue we must settle is not gaining more wisdom, or praying for more talents or gifts; it is not a larger IQ, or increasing our fame and trophies, in order to impress our mentorees. It is, instead, determining to make a *commitment to relationships.* No doubt, our ability to mentor or receive mentoring is increased through having greater gifts or a greater capacity for insight. But we cannot do anything about those things. We can, however, do something about our commitments. We must cross the "line in the sand" and commit to the mentoring process.

I wrote about this commitment in my handbook on the subject, called, *Mentoring: How to Invest Your Life in Others.* I described the three-fold commitment we must make:
- We must be committed to a PERSON
- We must be committed to a PROCESS
- We must be committed to a PURPOSE

These commitments are going to require us to possess patience, mercy, understanding, flexibility and perseverance—whether we are the mentor or the mentoree. Because mentoring involves the will of another human and all that comes with their human nature, there is likely to be some conflict, even if we really like them! At least part of the growth we'll experience in the process will come from the "rub" of being in relationship with another human being. This is all part of God's intentional plan for us. Let me explain.

EXPERIMENTING IN YOUR LABORATORY...

The kind of relationships created by mentoring and accountability are unique, indeed. They represent ideal growth places for us, almost like *families*, which are designed to foster growth in us. I refer to these places as relational "laboratories."

Do you remember science class, in college? Every science class (it seemed to me) had two components to them: a **lecture** and a **lab**. The lecture was the boring part; we had to sit and listen to someone lecture to us, from the text book. But the *lab* was the fun part! We got to actually experiment with test tubes and Bunsen burners—and "do the stuff" we only talked about in the lecture! Do you remember those days of exploding gases and boiling test tubes? The labs I participated in were nothing short of hilarious.

Now, here's the analogy. Laboratories, by definition, are supposed to be *safe places* to experiment. We can try those things we are only beginning to understand, because everybody understands we are *practicing*. We are not *experts!* The same can be said for mentoring relationships. They are relationship LABS! They are safe places to learn how to grow; to hold each other accountable with those habitual sin areas of our lives; to learn how to be vulnerable and confess our sins and shortcomings. They are safe places because the mentor and the mentoree have made a commitment not to walk away prematurely. There is a covenant, agreed upon by both parties.

It's the same thing that makes families work. Marriage and family are supposed to be safe places, ideally. They represent a *home* where people are not going to walk away, even when the kids are learning how to keep promises; or mom is learning how to balance her family and personal needs; or where dad is learning how to be an effective spiritual leader.

These are all portraits of *relational labs*, designed for us to grow in. Still to this day, I will make mistakes in our home, and have to say to my wife: "Honey... I am still in my laboratory!" And it's true. I am still experimenting. Thank God I have a godly, mature wife who forgives and allows me to learn and grow. I am safe.

All of us need these "labs." This is one reason why we all need mentoring relationships. Most of the world in which we live is *not* a safe place. I will encounter some 10,000 other relationships this year alone, many of which are with non-christians. They are people who are hurting, angry and sometimes fail to have ethics enough to prevent them from hurting others. Believe me, I need some safe places to love and be loved. Further, I am going to guess that you do, too. I am challenging you, now, to find your *laboratory!*

DECISION TIME...

We will make this decision intelligently, when we wrestle with the following questions. This is your decision time; your opportunity to seize the moment, and commit yourself to this wonderful, biblical process called mentoring. May I suggest three categories of questions, based upon the material in this devotional handbook:

I. REVIEW - WHICH OF THESE BIBLICAL "PORTRAITS" SPOKE TO YOU WITH *THE GREATEST AMOUNT OF RELEVANCE?*

A. What were the greatest lessons you learned from the mentorees? Who reminded you of *you?* Why do you suppose you identified with these mentorees?

B. What were the greatest lessons you learned from the mentors?

What kind of mentors were they, according to the definitions listed in chapter one? (Were they disciplers, coaches, teachers, etc.)

C. What specific applications can you make today?

I trust it is clear to you, after reflecting on the answers to these questions above, that we can actually be mentored *long distance* by those who do not live near us, nor live in our own lifetime! Mentors can invest in us through the written word, especially from the pages of scripture. Hebrews 11 reminds us that all of these godly folks in the Old Testament are written about to be examples to us, today! We can be mentored from the past. In addition, the scripture gives us clear illustrations of the danger of *not* having a mentor in our lives. Consider the life of Samson—who had an influential position as judge in Israel, but had no one guiding him, helping him to get a handle on his fleshly appetites? He is a vivid example of a poor leader... who desperately needed a mentor.

Eli, while he did prove that he could prepare young Samuel for the priesthood, could have used a godly mentor to speak into his life, regarding his family. His own sons were an abomination to God. He had confused priorities, but didn't learn this until it was too late. And how about Absolom? King David wasn't able to restrain him from personal rebellion and ruin—even though he was Absolom's father. What a marvelous opportunity David missed when he failed to mentor Absolom. On the other hand, perhaps he did try to do so, but never got a teachable response from his son. If this were the case—what a marvelous opportunity Absolom missed because he would not be mentored!

Think about it. Although this book has just outlined thirty-two successful mentoring relationships in the scriptures, there seems to be just as many failures at the process. In addition to the ones I've just mentioned, consider Adam and Cain: the story of a son who desperately needed some guidance in controlling his ego and emotions. Somehow, he and Adam never connected at this crucial level. Or, consider how King Saul failed to listen to his *potential mentor* Samuel. Saul might have been able to remain as king of Israel, if he'd only submitted to a godly mentor. The same is true for the sons of Eli, the priest; and for Demus, who failed to listen to the Apostle Paul—and left the faith for his worldly passions. Evidently, no one had enough authority or intimacy to help him sift through his fleshly desires to draw the right conclusions. There is danger when we fail to enter into strong mentoring relationships.

II. REMEMBER - WHO HAVE BEEN *THE GREATEST INFLUENCES* ON YOUR LIFE, THUS FAR?

A. How did they gain influence, or mentor you? (Was it intentional on their part?)

B. What qualities gave them such influence in your life?

C. Which of these traits can you reproduce in others?

As I put these thoughts down on paper, I have reflected on those "influential" people in my own life. Although there have probably been hundreds of them, I can specifically think of ten who've left their spiritual "fingerprints" on my life:

1. *My parents* (who gave me everything)
2. *Mrs. Mayo* (my elementary teacher)
3. *Shawn Mitchell* (my high school friend/mentor)
4. *Mr. Mosher* (my high school teacher)
5. *Jim Sullivan* (my youth group director)
6. *Mike Muccio* (college friend/mentor)
7. *Evangelists* (long distance mentors)
8. *Bob Stamps* (my college chaplain)
9. *Missions strategists* (distant mentors)
10. *John Maxwell* (my employer/mentor)

In addition to these, I have my fellow travelers at Kingdom Building Ministries, many of whom have become "peer mentors" and comrades in the journey. Steve and Dwight, for instance, are good friends who are at similar places in their own spiritual pilgrimage.

As I ponder these names listed above, I find some interesting tidbits to note. First, some of these relationships were *long term;* others were very short lived. Consequently, I have noticed (in my life) that impact doesn't necessarily require years and years of time, but rather being in my life *at the right time!* Second, while most were cross-generational, (being a generation or two older than I was), others were "peer mentors" who seemed to be at "similar places" in their own journeys. I think we need both. Third, some were males and others were females. This was interesting for me to note. No doubt, I believe that it is best to meet with a mentor from the same gender. At the same time, however, some of the women in my life have shown me truths about God that only women can reveal. For instance, there is a mothering, nurturing side of God's nature that females demonstrate so naturally. My own wife has taught me things about God I would have never caught on my own. Finally, these people represented various relationships and authority to me. Some were teachers, some were friends; some were in God-given positions of authority over me, while others—I invited in myself, simply because I respected them. Clearly, mentors can be found almost anywhere, if we'll open our eyes to learn and observe.

III. RESPOND - How Can You Participate In This Long, Historical Line Of Mentoring?

A. What is *your* next step? Do you need to find another mentor? If so, what kind of mentor do you need: a coach, a guide, a teacher, etc.? Are you ready to look for a mentoree? Where is a logical place to find one?

B. What is your chief contribution to make, based on who you are? In other words, what do you have to offer someone else, in a mentoring relationship?

C. Who might you establish an accountable relationship with, now? Are there any "peer mentors" in your life? Why not start investing in some today?

The decision that awaits you is simply this: Will you stop merely "spending your time" and begin "investing your life"? So much of our lives we waste "living life on accident" instead of "living life on purpose." There are few things you could do that are more purposeful than to enter an intentional, mentoring relationship.

As you ponder the idea of investing in someone, let me make the following suggestions:

1. **SET THE DIRECTION.** Don't allow the time you invest to simply drift. Be intentional about what you discuss and where you feel they need to go. Fix in your mind that you are to *coach who they are becoming.* The best way to approach this is to follow the counsel of Father Hesberg, a catholic priest, who said: "Be honest, be human, be humble." Bring with you specific questions you are going to ask your mentoree (or your mentor), when you meet. Gain permission from them to move in this direction—then, go for it.

2. **POSSESS GOALS.** Mutually decide what they are to accomplish, in the different areas which you are holding them accountable. Make these goals measurable, and set a completion date. Make sure they are items that they can work on *right now!* William James once said that most humans only accomplish about 15% of their potential. I believe this is because we don't have mentors who help us set and hit our targets. In all of this, however, remember: you are not working for greatness but for progress.

3. **BECOME THEIR BIGGEST FAN.** This will enable you to foster their growth. You desire their success; you want them to win. Affirm any step forward they take. Encourage them when they've fallen short. This will increase your authority in their life, and give your words greater weight when you speak in the future. Visualize them becoming all that they can be, but in the process— stay patient, stay persistent and stay personal.

4. **MODEL THE LIFE YOU WANT FOR THEM.** Do you remember the principle discussed in the model of David, as he mentored his mighty men in the cave of Adullam? *People do what people see.* No matter what great sermons you're able to pull out of your hat, or how eloquent you expound on biblical truth—your mentoree is going to watch how you "flesh" it out, and copy your example. Whatever you demonstrate, good or bad, will likely be emulated by those who follow you. If you are a parent—you've seen this

prnciple in reality. Children may hear you say, "Be honest!" but if, when the phone rings, you say, "Tell them I'm not here!"—how do you think they are going to define honesty from your life? Remember, Christian faith and ministry is like a disease: it is more *caught* than *taught*.

MY OBSERVATIONS AND EXPERIENCE...

I have noticed some consistent truths over time, whether observing mentors and mentorees in the Bible, or in my own life experience. Look these over, and be encouraged as you pace yourself in your own mentoring relationships. This list of observations is helpful for both mentors and mentorees:

1. *Progress is almost always slower than you'd like.*
2. *Growth usually happens like this: Climb...then plateau. Climb...then plateau, again.*
3. *We should give people options, not advice. We can't make decisions for them.*
4. *There is always a midway point in the mentoring process where we are tempted to quit.*
5. *We must always keep the person's vision and goals clear, and remind them of it.*
6. *We're attracted to the other person's strengths, but must live with their weaknesses.*
7. *We must reap something despite differences/faults: eat the fish and spit out the bones.*
8. *We must build "standers" not "leaners"- Get the job done then let them move on.*

A HEALTHY CONCLUSION...

I hope this chapter has given you incentive to "get connected" to a mentor or mentoree. Each of us needs accountability and support, relationally. As I have mentioned earlier: we need each other. We have seen this exhibited through the mentoring relationships in the scripture. We hear the cry for it today from the disconnected people of our generation. Let me close this one with a simple yet colorful challenge from the pen of Robert Fulgam, author of *All I Really Need to Know I Learned in Kindergarten.* In this book, he remembers playing "hide and seek" as a boy, growing up. He reflected on those days as a game of "hide and seek" was taking place in front of him, in his neighborhood. Listen to his reflections and hear his plea:

Did you have a kid in your neighborhood who always hid so good, nobody could find him? We did. After a while we would give up on him and go off, leaving him to rot wherever he was. Sooner or later he would show up, all mad because we didn't keep looking for him. And we would be mad back because he wasn't playing the game the way it was supposed to be played. There's *hiding* and there's *finding,* we'd say. And he'd say it was hide-and-seek, not hide-and-give-UP, and we'd all yell about who made the rules and who cared about who anyway, and how we wouldn't play with him anymore if he didn't get it straight and who needed him anyhow, and things like that. Hide-and-seek-and-yell. No matter what, though, the next time he would hide too good again. He's probably still hidden somewhere, for all I know.

As I write this, the neighborhood game goes on, and there is a kid under a pile of leaves in the yard just under my window. He has been there for a long time now, and everybody else is found and they are about to give up on him over at the base. I considered going out to the base and telling them where he is hiding. And I thought about setting the leaves on fire to drive him out. Finally, I just yelled, "GET FOUND KID!" out the window. And scared him so bad he probably wet his pants and started crying and ran home to tell his mother. It's real hard to know how to be helpful sometimes.

A man I know found out last year he had terminal cancer. He was a doctor. And knew about dying, and he didn't want to make his family and friends suffer through that with him. So he kept his secret. And died. Everybody said how brave he was to bear his suffering in silence and not tell everybody, and so on and so forth. But privately his family and friends said how angry they were that he didn't need them, didn't trust their strength. And it hurt that he didn't say good-bye.

He hid too well. Getting found would have kept him in the game. Hide-and-seek, grown up style. Wanting to hide. Needing to be sought. Confused about being found. "I don't want anyone to know." "What will people think?" "I don't want to bother anyone."

Better than hide-and-seek, I like the game called: Sardines. In Sardines the person who is It goes and hides, and everybody goes looking for him. When you find him, you get in with him and hide there with him. Pretty soon everybody is hiding together, all stacked in a small place like puppies in a pile. And pretty soon somebody giggles and somebody laughs and everybody gets found.

Medieval theologians even described God in hide-and-seek terms, calling Him *Deus Absconditus.* But me, I think God is a Sardine player. And will be found the same way everybody gets found in Sardines—by the sound of laughter of those heaped together at the end.

"Olly-olly-oxen-free." The kids out in the street are hollering the cry that says "Come on in, wherever you are. It's a new game." And so say I. To all those who have hid too good. *Get found kid!* Olly-olly-oxen-free.

Good words. And I close with them. Why not go and "get found." You have just read about thirty-two developmental relationships that God used to change the world. Why not go and begin to write the story of number thirty-three? It's your move.

ABOUT KINGDOM BUILDING MINISTRIES

The mission of Kingdom Building Ministries (KBM) is to partner with the body of Christ to raise up new generations of laborers for Kingdom service worldwide.

The vision of KBM is to raise up one million laborers by the year 2004 who become catalysts for movements of prayer, growth in the local church, and the completion of the task of world evangelism.

CORE VALUES:

Laborers - More than numerical church growth, laborers are the greatest need for worldwide harvest.

Prayer - Human effort is not enough, intercessory prayer is Jesus' strategy for raising up laborers.

Mentoring - True laborers cannot be mass produced, they are raised up through life on life mentoring.

Multiplication - Addition falls short, spiritual multiplication is the only way to raise laborers in sufficient numbers.

KBM is committed to preparing people to enter their field of ministry, whether it is as a full-time, vocational worker, or as a layperson. Each of us has a calling and a purpose from God to fulfill in our lives. Our commitment to prepare you includes:

• **Itinerant Speakers.** KBM has men and women who desire to share with your church, retreat or campus how to live out Kingdom values in today's world.

• **Additional Resources.** There are many books and tape series available from KBM on Kingdom issues. Designed to prepare individuals for service, topics include mentoring, missions, and others.

• **The Laborers Network (TLN).** The Laborer's Network couples laborers with a local mentor for twelve lessons and application exercises. The training is practical and equips the laborer to be a multiplier.

• **The Laborers Institute (TLI).** The Laborer's Institute is our three month training school, allowing the laborer to develop deeper spiritual disciplines and receive training in various ministry avenues.

For more information on these and other opportunities available through Kingdom Building Ministries, call or write to us at:

Kingdom Building Ministries
14140 East Evans Avenue
Denver, CO 80014
E-mail: Laborers@aol.com
1-800-873-8957